English Solutions

Teacher's Guide A

for books 1–3

Jim Sweetman

LONGMAN

Longman Group Limited

Longman House, Burnt Mill, Harlow, Essex CM20 2JE, England and Associated Companies throughout the World.

First published 1995
© Longman Group Ltd 1995

Typeset in New Century Schoolbook by GreenGate Publishing Services, Tonbridge, Kent
Printed in the UK by York Publishing Services

ISBN 0582 265762

The publisher's policy is to use paper manufactured from sustainable forests.

Contents

Book 2

Introduction

Dear Colleague,

This guide is short, practical and to the point. It is designed to help you plan schemes of work and your lessons from day to day. It offers advice on the use of *English Solutions* books 1–3 in a direct, straightforward way.

The copymasters provide copies of the student charts in *English Solutions* and offer additional resources for students across the ability range. Quality of learning and differentiation are key words in OFSTED inspection and these materials are planned to help teachers to demonstrate their commitment to both of these through their own good practice.

The writing of *English Solutions* has been monitored by a team of expert readers and over a hundred classroom teachers have commented on sample extracts. Their observations have helped to shape the material in valuable ways and their contribution is gratefully acknowledged.

With best wishes,

1 The English curriculum

The National Curriculum for English

The English curriculum has changed fundamentally. It now consists of three attainment targets – Speaking & Listening, Reading and Writing. To all intents and purposes, these are equally weighted at Key Stages 1–3. Speaking & Listening incorporates the performance of standard English in appropriate contexts. Reading specifies some pre-twentieth century writers and Writing includes the features of spelling and handwriting that were previously separated out as presentation.

Attainment targets

The attainment targets are described in similar terms at each key stage. An overall description is followed by a statement about range and progression from the previous stage. That is followed by a description of key skills and a comment on standard English and language study.

Level descriptions

Level descriptions have replaced statements of attainment. These are clearly identified with assessment at the end of a key stage. Each level description is an account of the characteristic features of a student's performance at that level. Level descriptions are designed to be applied to completed work in order to give an indication of its achievement. The effect is to elevate the key skills to a new importance.

Key skills

The curriculum was designed to avoid accusations of curriculum fragmentation or 'box ticking'. This makes the requirements more opaque than in previous versions. While the change gives teachers more freedom, it may also make them less secure about whether their teaching is in line with what the curriculum requires.

The key skills section for each attainment target at each key stage sets out the framework within which teachers should work. It describes skills as inter-related rather than discrete and views them as competencies to be re-visited rather than as hurdles to be mastered and forgotten. In fact, the curriculum urges teachers not to try to separate out the curriculum into a range of skills. It contains no overall list of key skills against which teachers can check their schemes of work; and the way that skills are covered at one key stage rather than another is not mapped out. The reasons for this are clear but it can lead to some confusion.

So, what are the key skill areas in the new curriculum? The charts on the following pages show, for each attainment target and in summary form, one version of the key skills that should be taught to, or developed in, pupils at Key Stages 3 and 4. They also illustrate some of the classroom activities that might meet these requirements.

SPEAKING & LISTENING ▬▬▬▬▬▬▬▬▬▬

Using standard English where appropriate, pupils should be taught to:

KEY SKILLS	ACTIVITIES
1 Contribute in discussion • adapt speech to listeners and activity • take other speakers' views into account • cite evidence to support an opinion • argue persuasively	• talking as a whole class, in small groups or pairs in response to stimuli, or for a set purpose • brainstorming ideas • giving explanation, description or narration • role play
2 Structure talk for an audience • select appropriate level • use discourse markers • use gesture and intonation	Using standard English where appropriate • reporting back to the class • giving a short talk to the group • giving a public presentation • making a speech • take part in a scripted performance
3 Respond and restructure • ask and answer questions • summarise what has been said • identify salient points • clarify and synthesise the ideas of others • modify their ideas	• taking an active role in class, group and pair discussion • acting as chairperson for a group or meeting • replying in public debate • exploring ideas and hypotheses • arguing, debating and persuading • analysing issues • conducting interviews
4 Reach conclusions through discussion • identify consensus • negotiate agreement • agree to differ	• forming an opinion on an issue • deciding on a course of action • talking about literature and the media • role playing and improvisation • developing ideas
5 Listen carefully and positively • note features of talk – tone, undertone, implication • note a speaker's intentions through verbal / non-verbal clues • note ambiguities, vagueness and glossing of points	• noting features of language in commenting on other speakers, audiotapes and videos • understanding and anticipating a speaker's intentions • acting as recorder and reporting back to the class • viewing, and responding to, films and television programmes • conducting a survey
6 Understand the development of language • note how languages change over time • understand word origins • understand the differences between speech and writing, and between dialects	• talking about their own language use and that of others • commenting on dialects and other forms of language • finding word origins and discussing language change

READING

Pupils should be taught to:

KEY SKILLS	ACTIVITIES
1 Engage with content and language in all their reading • infer meaning • develop insights and opinions • select material • follow arguments • develop an understanding of genre • analyse authorial techniques • compare language use across media • read texts from other cultures	In speech or writing: • elucidating complex meanings • comparing texts • answering comprehension exercises • analysing writing types and authorial standpoints • retrieving information and arguments • analysing reading in relation to other media • exploring attitudes and values in texts
2 Read narrative • read a wide variety of texts independently and for enjoyment • read, and appreciate the qualities of, prescribed works by significant authors • distinguish the different attitudes of characters and writers • describe character, plot and effect on a reader • understand the characteristics of literary language and styles	In speech or writing: • reacting to literary texts • offering critical commentaries • comparing texts • analysing literary genres • 'hot-seating' characters In writing: • answering comprehension questions • giving empathic accounts • responding to, or developing, adaptations • writing creatively in response to reading
3 Read plays • understand and appreciate drama as performance • read, and appreciate the qualities of, prescribed works by significant authors • identify variety in structure and setting • respond to key ideas, themes and messages • describe character, plot and effect on a reader • appreciate the richness and diversity of language use	
4 Read poetry • read, and appreciate the qualities of, prescribed works by significant authors • understand about possible forms and styles • appreciate the richness and diversity of language use	
5 Respond to factual and informative texts • read, and appreciate the qualities of, a wide range of non-fiction texts • understand the characteristics of media texts • select information • compare and synthesise information • make effective use of relevant information • evaluate the presentation of information • distinguish fact, opinion and bias • note distinctive features of vocabulary and grammar	In speech or writing: • describing features of non-literary texts • commenting on and analysing types of non-literary text • researching information for writing In writing: • writing discursively or argumentatively in response to texts • writing opinion and persuasion based on reading

WRITING

Pupils should be taught to:

KEY SKILLS	ACTIVITIES
1 Understand the writing process • plan complex tasks • draft and redraft on paper and screen • proof-read accurately	• note-making • drafting and redrafting • proof-reading and revising
2 Understand and use standard English • understand the functions of phrases, main and subordinate clauses and sentence structure • appreciate discourse structure • understand the functions of parts of speech • analyse language use in their own writing • punctuate effectively and accurately using the full range of punctuation marks	• analysing grammar and punctuation • practice exercises • writing in literary and non-literary forms in formal and informal ways or for a set audience
3 Write narrative • write narratives based on reading and personal experience • structure settings, characterisation and plot • distinguish different forms of narrative writing	• writing different forms of narrative including diaries, biography, stories and screenplays • writing imaginative stories, stories based on reading and empathic narratives • describing characters • preparing adaptations
4 Write script • write playscripts based on reading, performance and personal experience • use dialogue to convey character	• writing imaginative playscripts • adapting role plays into script • preparing adaptations of read materials • writing media treatments based on texts
5 Write poetry • write poems based on reading and personal experience • understand and practise poetic forms • introduce poetic devices into own writing	• writing poetry in different forms • using poetic language and effects in their own writing
6 Write in non-literary ways • understand different forms of non-fiction writing including discursive, argumentative and persuasive types • write informatively drawing on a range of reading and research	• writing for discursive, argumentative and persuasive purposes • writing reports, letters, articles, notes, case studies, projects and topics • presenting information for different purposes and audiences • writing analyses and commentaries on non-literary texts
7 Use presentational devices • write neatly and legibly • understand and use appropriate text features	• designing pages using layout and text effects • using handwriting for decorative or artistic purposes • using WP and DTP facilities for effect
8 Spell correctly • spell complex and irregular words • use a dictionary	• proof-reading and revising • correction exercises • test the learning of spelling rules

2 Using English Solutions in the classroom

English Solutions and the National Curriculum

Each book in the *English Solutions* series for Key Stage 3 provides a year's work in English for students in Years 7–9. This assumes that the book will be supported by other related activities and the reading of whole texts – stories, poems and plays. Taken together, the three books cover the key skills required by the National Curriculum at Key Stage 3 and provide an overall scheme of work for the key stage.

Wherever possible, the three attainment targets – speaking & listening, reading and writing – are connected. A skills model with Target boxes, Skills boxes and Tips boxes underpins the books, but it is never allowed to overwhelm the central focus of the unit.

All the reading requirements of the curriculum have been meticulously accommodated but the range of reading has not been curtailed. Alongside pre-twentieth century authors, the books feature contemporary material, much of which is new and has not been previously anthologized.

The books do not, and should not, replace the teacher. They are designed to support teachers in their work, to bring variety into the classroom and to assist with the development of programmes of study, assessment and the recording of achievement.

The units

There are 32 units in books 1–3. While their outline structure is identical, the units differ in length, organisation and the demands they make on pupils. Variety in all of these areas is built into the course. Some units are not only longer on the page but will take more time to complete in the classroom. Others are deliberately designed to be short exercises. Some units start with reading, others start with speech. Most, but not all, present an increasing level of demand on the student. These variations are brought out in the commentaries on each unit in this Guide. However, the Target boxes, the Tips boxes and Skills boxes are common features that link the separate units and underline how the books are designed to develop progression in English.

Teachers use books like these in different ways according to circumstances. Apart from the normal teaching programme within a school, there is often a need to cover lessons for colleagues attending in-service meetings or for sickness. Alterations to the school timetable caused by examinations and interviews can also mean that single lessons have to be covered at short notice. The pattern of school terms can also make more – or less – time available.

To meet these different needs, each book contains some units that are almost entirely stand alone, or can be completed – albeit at a minimal level – with little teacher supervision and within a relatively short space of time. There are also many activities within the units that can be set independently to cover single lessons.

Key skills and progression

A progressive model underpins the series combined with the regular revisiting of important skills. Each book has a teacher's matrix, which lists the key skills that are being practised in every unit and this Guide indicates the areas where teachers should hope to find evidence of student progression.

Key skills and progression are pivotal terms in the English curriculum. The message is not that English can be reduced to a list of basic skills but that the subject is made up of overlapping competencies that can be visited at a range of levels. For example, the key ability to write narrative is encouraged by reading, advice on techniques and an understanding of narrative techniques. The form of teaching used depends on the age of the class and the abilities of the students. It is important to stress that there are no clear hierarchies within this framework and that the activities that develop the key skills are not intended to develop them discretely.

To put it simply, if the old curriculum had the structure of a family tree, the new curriculum is now circular.

In a sense, this approach reflects what English teachers have always practised. The rehearsal and revisiting of skills within a framework of Speaking & Listening, Reading and Writing is at the heart of any English teacher's personal notion of the curriculum. The approach only differs in that the key skills are more carefully spelt out at each key stage. In this Guide the key skills involved in each unit are represented by letters on the first page of the teacher's notes for the unit:

(S&L) Speaking & listening

(R) Reading

(W) Writing

English Solutions and the Scottish Curriculum

The units provided in *English Solutions* will help Scottish teachers to meet the demands of the curriculum at the upper stages of primary schools and in the first and second years of secondary schools. The materials take account of the principles that underpin *English Language 5–14* and *Standard Grade*, principles that highlight the need for breadth, balance, differentiation and progression within a curriculum designed to meet the needs, and reflect the interests, of individual pupils.

Both *English Language 5–14* and *Standard Grade* encourage teachers to provide a broad and balanced curriculum. Both encourage teachers to take account of the interdependence of the four modes, listening, talking, reading and writing and to consider individual needs by providing challenging assignments that allow pupils to develop their language skills at their own pace. The units in *English Solutions* provide a range of contexts to help teachers translate these demands into effective classroom practice. Varied material offers teachers and pupils choices both about the stimulus and the assignments they undertake.

Throughout the series, the holistic framework reflects the requirements in *English Language 5–14* and *Standard Grade* to provide pupils with opportunities to study an extensive range of texts and explore them through activities in each of the language modes. The imaginative approaches to assessment which are explicit in the Scottish curriculum guidelines are clearly reflected in the units found in *English Solutions*. Within each of these, there is a range of methods including teacher, self, paired and group assessment. Different ways of gathering assessment evidence are also explored including pupils logs and diaries as recommended in *English Language 5–14*.

English Solutions, by providing a variety of exciting contexts for teaching and learning will prove to be an invaluable teaching resource for teachers as they work to meet the specific demands of the Scottish curriculum.

English Solutions and the Curriculum for Northern Ireland

Teachers will welcome the format of both pupil books and the Teachers' Guide in *English Solutions*. The assignments provide a wide range of relevant content and activities that range across the three attainment targets for teachers following the English curriculum for Northern Ireland.

The emphasis on a comparative approach to texts introduces activities that are excellent preparation for the current NISEAC GCSE syllabuses while the concern to stress Knowledge about Language, informational texts, drama and presentational skills mirrors many of the current concerns among teachers in Northern Ireland.

In some units, extracts are interrupted by activities demanding reflection, analysis and prediction. In these, teachers will find similarities with some of the best practice of the Assessment Units for Key Stage 3.

UNITS THAT CAN BE USED ON A STAND ALONE BASIS TO COVER TEACHER ABSENCE FOR A WEEK OR MORE

Unit		Page	Comments
Book 1	A day out	46	Needs a brief introduction and (helpfully) copymasters from the Teacher's Guide. Also ask for a written version of the talk (page 53).
	Tomb of the lost pharaoh	108	There are six pieces of written work (a list of items, a letter, a description, a journal entry, a script and a newspaper article) to complete and a map to be drawn.
Book 2	Who's at home?	56	This is a short unit that could be covered in a week of lessons by a supply teacher.
	The egg-man	62	The narrative in this unit can be read over the course of a few lessons and the tasks on pages 64, 68 and 73 completed.
Book 3	The Harry Hastings method	70	This unit can be completed by a class with a supply teacher in about a week.
	Animal crackers	126	The second half of the unit from pages 132 to 137 can be used by a class working independently.

UNITS THAT CAN BE USED TO COVER SINGLE/DOUBLE LESSONS

Unit		Page	Comments
Book 1	My top ten	12	Read pages 8–12 and complete task 4 on page 12.
	Body rhythms	32	Complete the task on page 33, writing about **two** of the faces illustrated.
	It's a small world		Read *The Little Man* (pages 57–59) and write answers to the questions that follow.
Book 2	A day in your life	8	Use the information on page 16 to write about a day in your life.
	A matter of taste	76	Read pages 76–79 and then write your own menu by completing the task on page 79.
	Stranded	92	Read the extracts on pages 95–101 and write answers to the questions on page 101.
Book 3	Listen up!	8	Complete the questionnaire on pages 9 and 10. Then write a short commentary saying what it revealed about you and whether you agree with it.
	Animal characters	24	Read the extract from *Black Beauty* on pages 34–37 and write your answers to the questions on page 37.
	Good friends	102	Read the extract from *Tom Sawyer* on pages 104–107. Make neat copies of – and complete – the two charts on page 107.

UNITS THAT CAN BE USED TO COVER SINGLE/DOUBLE LESSONS

My top ten

AIMS

✔ This is a simple unit involving opportunities for collaborative work.

✔ The unit is ideal for the beginning of a new school year because it encourages students – who may or may not know one another – to work together in an area that is not strictly academic, where every student can have something to contribute.

✔ The basic framework can be expanded to allow a new teacher with a new class to undertake some preliminary diagnosis of strengths and weaknesses.

✔ With a familiar group, or more able students, the need to justify preferences and choices in speech and writing takes the unit on to a higher level.

ADDITIONAL RESOURCES

These include other top ten charts (very popular with Sunday newspaper supplements and all sorts of magazines). There are also various books of lists, but some of these may be too esoteric for this level.

Large sheets of paper and marker pens will be useful for the group sessions.

KEY SKILLS

(S&L) Contribute in discussion

(S&L) Reach conclusions through discussion

(W) Write in non-literary ways – giving an opinion

This unit develops skills in Speaking & Listening that are appropriate to this key stage. The context for talk is made deliberately simple. However, the role of the chair is an important one where individuals can show higher level skills.

Writing about preferences is a sophisticated form of writing, here approached at a basic level.

PROGRESSION

Look for individual student progression in these areas:

● an ability to work confidently with a group

● competence in the management of small group discussion

● the confidence to encourage consensus or to handle disagreement

● the ability to listen to what others are saying in defining the consensus

● the ability to develop an opinion in writing through supported argument.

USING THE UNIT IN THE CLASSROOM

1 Write your own top ten

2 Make a class display

With a new class, arrange the seating to suit yourself. Introduce the topic then ask the students to note down their lists before there is any discussion. The talk that follows is then focused on paper and is likely to be less embarrassing. Encouraging the students to talk to the person next to them may be the best way into this exercise. Then, sharing lists with people who chose the same subject for their lists will help to integrate the class. Homework could be to find another top ten over a weekend and to use this to start the class display. Copymaster 1 is supplied to help with this.

3 Discuss in a group

There are two new roles here: the chair and a note-taker who reports back to the class. You may need to intervene in these appointments or you may find that the group has a clearer idea than you have of who is suitable. Keep the reporting back brief.

4 Write about your choices

This is the first opportunity to introduce the class to the use of Skills boxes in *English Solutions*. Here the box takes students through the National Curriculum writing model:

- Plan
- Draft
- Revise
- Proof-read
- Present.

Stress that this is a model for writing in general. Working with partners or in small groups will be helpful. This is also a chance to establish your ground rules for writing in the classroom in terms of quiet periods, calling out and proof-reading.

5 Reach an agreement and report back

This discussion is more demanding. You may find it helpful to treat the first task as a class exercise with you at the front while the students brainstorm some ideas. That will lead on to the more demanding task that follows. Ask for a different person to report back.

6 Make a list of what really matters

This activity can be approached quite briefly as a class exercise but it offers the opportunity for some more personal writing. If the school encourages pupil journals, this is an ideal way to start one. Alternatively, it could be a homework task. Make clear that this does not have to be a long piece of writing.

There is a chance here to make connections with the PSE or tutorial programme in the school. Doing this at an early stage, emphasises for the class that teachers do work together and talk to one another!

A writing template (Copymaster 3) is provided for students with learning difficulties.

EXTENDING THE UNIT

1 Write another list

Write a list of your top ten favourite books. Explain your top three choices.

2 Write in more detail about your choices

Select any one of your 'lists' and write in detail about what influenced *your* choices

3 Carry out a survey

Organise a simple survey to find a class top ten using the activity sheet (Copymaster 2).

4 Compare what people think

Ask an older person and a younger person to give you their top ten television programmes. Compare their choices.

My top ten

```
┌──────────────────────────────────────────────┐
│                                                │
│                                                │
└──────────────────────────────────────────────┘
```

```
        ┌────────────────────────────────┐
        │              By                │
        │                                │
        └────────────────────────────────┘
```

1 _____

2 _____

3 _____

4 _____

5 _____

6 _____

7 _____

8 _____

9 _____

10 _____

English Solutions   © Longman Group Limited 1995   **Book 1 unit 1**

My top ten
Favourite foods survey

Use this questionnaire to carry out a simple survey of your family and friends. At the side of the grid, note down the possible choices. These could be things you have for tea (macaroni cheese, beans on toast, beefburgers and so on), favourite sweets, favourite ice-cream flavours, breakfast cereals and so on.

Along the top of the grid, write in the names of the ten people you speak to. Ask them for their first three choices from your list and put 1, 2 or 3 in the box for that choice under their names. Put a 4 in all the other boxes in that column.

To work out the top three favourites add the totals in each row. The lowest total is the favourite, the second lowest is second favourite and the third lowest is number three.

Foods	Names of the people you asked										Totals	Winners

English Solutions   © Longman Group Limited 1995   **Book l unit l**

MY TOP TEN OF

[   ]

The top ten I have chosen to write about is my top ten of

_____

I chose to write about this top ten because

_____
_____

In my writing, I am going to say something about my top three choices, starting with number three. My third choice is

_____

I chose this because

_____
_____

My second choice is

_____

I chose this because

_____
_____

My top choice is

_____

I selected this as my top choice because

_____
_____

These are my choices now but I expect they will change because

_____
_____

How it all began

AIMS

✔ This unit starts with a familiar theme but presents an unusual range of accessible stimulus material.

✔ The unit is open-ended with plenty of opportunity for extension. It allows individuals in a new class to show the teacher their capabilities

✔ The materials link with the teaching of religious education and art.

ADDITIONAL RESOURCES

Other creation stories from a range of cultures can be introduced to the class. Pupils can also be asked to seek out further stories for themselves.

KEY SKILLS

(S&L) Structure a talk for an audience – retelling a story

(S&L) Listen carefully and positively

(R) Engage with content and language – compare creation stories

(W) Write narrative

The range of reading here, although quite demanding, is appropriate to the key stage. Writing the stories requires some perception of genre.

PROGRESSION

Look for individual student progression in these areas:

• the ability to make inferences and generalise about the stories in discussion

• a developing competence in drama and performance

• an increased understanding of the importance of audience in dramatic retelling and writing.

USING THE UNIT

This unit focuses on creation stories – stories that explain how things are in the present by reference to events, or supposed events, in the past. In doing this, it incorporates elements of myth and legend and touches on events that have religious significance. In this last regard, the subject requires sensitive handling in the classroom.

1 Reading creation stories

One way to introduce the unit is to ask the class about how the Earth was formed. Ask who, or what, was the prime mover. Talk about the unexplainable and how there is a need in human beings to try to explain what cannot be understood. Point out that for primitive peoples that need was even greater.

Mention some of the alternative proposals. Ancient Chinese myth describes the early world as the yolk in an egg where the sky is the inside of the shell. Hindu stories also say that the universe came from an egg – this time one made up of gold and silver fragments.

Chinese myth saw the sky as supported on pillars that allowed it to rotate above the Earth – thereby explaining the movement of the stars. A sophisticated version argues that a monster displaced the north-western pillar so that the sky now sags in that direction. This explains the tilt in the Earth and why the great rivers of China flow in one direction. Natural events such as earthquakes, storms and eclipses have also often been explained by arguments between angry gods or as battles between the sky and earth.

It is probably best to read the version of Genesis to the class. It is a powerful text and repays a dramatic reading. That will allow you to talk briefly about how the Bible explains the origins of humanity and the Earth before going on to read the other extracts.

The discussion that follows should be wide-ranging but some groups may require prompting and a longer reporting back session. Use your experience of the class to allocate individuals to groups for the next session.

2 Retell a creation story

Retelling a story offers the chance to make these stories relevant to the students. The possibilities for drama should not be neglected and the final versions can be as polished as time allows. What is important is the sense of preparing material for an audience and the Tips box emphasises this aspect. With pupils who quickly appreciate the task, ask different groups to approach the story in distinct ways – mime, with voices, costume and so on. As with any such task, do not overlook the chance to show the finished product to an assembly or to younger pupils.

3 Look in detail at a creation story

The story of the cow and the giant contains many of the typical elements of a creation story. It also conveys the callousness and arbitrary nature of the activities that led to the formation of the world where man is perhaps only a minor element. Again, a dramatic reading will enhance the subsequent discussion. For some students, this task could be written, or could end with writing.

4 Write your own creation story

This is the main task in this unit. It reinforces the National Curriculum model of the writing process – plan, draft and proof-read – and specifies an audience. Encourage the group to start by setting their own questions based on the natural world. Where do the stars come from? What is snow? How do you explain a tornado? These are the kinds of questions to pose. You may be able to use a local geographical feature to give the story extra colour.

Encourage the group to imitate the style of the stories they have read. You could point out how the stories are often complicated and follow convoluted plots to get to their explanations but also note how they not only explain the creation of something but do so in a way that draws on its best known features.

Reading the best stories aloud will help to underline this.

EXTENDING THE UNIT

1 Researching other creation stories

Use the library to help you find other creation stories from other countries and cultures. Report back on one of them to the class by retelling a story and saying where it comes from. Copymaster 4 will help you.

2 Comparing the stories you have found

Use Copymaster 5 to contrast the stories you find and to see where they are similar.

3 Make a radio programme

Dramatise one of the creation stories for radio, using different voices for effect.

4 Draw a comic strip

Turn one of the stories into a colourful comic strip.

5 Modern myths

Find out something about the Bermuda Triangle, UFO sightings or corn circles. Write your own story that explains the phenomenon you have chosen.

6 Find a scientific answer

Find out what you can about the formation of the universe. Write a scientific explanation for young children.

How it all began
Finding other stories

Finding out more?

Use this sheet to record the details of another creation story and how you found out about it. First, you have to decide what information are you looking for. This should be your starting point. In your own words, note down exactly what you are looking for:

_____

_____

_____

_____

Finding information

Start with your school or local library. Ask the librarian to help you or use the library index. You may find something about these stories in fiction books which retell them, in the section on religion or in an encyclopaedia. Your RE teacher may also be able to help you. Note down what you did.

_____

_____

_____

_____

Selecting information

You should find plenty of material quite easily. First, **skim** through what you have found. This means read it quickly and decide whether it will be useful. Note down the books you looked at and the stories you found.

_____

_____

_____

_____

_____

Recording information

Make some notes or write your draft version of the story you are going to retell. Try to avoid copying out large amounts of information. **Use another sheet of paper for this.**

CM4

How it all began
Analysing creation myths

With your group, look at how the creation stories you have found are similar and at how they differ from one another.

Fill in this chart. One of the group could write or you could take it in turns, but all of you will be brainstorming the ideas to go into the chart.

Story name	Main features of the story	Similarities with other creation stories	Differences from other creation stories

English Solutions   © Longman Group Limited 1995   **Book 1 unit 2**

Body rhythms

AIMS

✔ This unit introduces the study of thematically linked poems.

✔ It presents an anthology of pre-twentieth century and contemporary poetry that can be approached in a number of ways.

✔ It challenges students to discuss what poetry is and encourages them to write their own poems.

ADDITIONAL RESOURCES

Other poems on the same theme will be useful. If the best examples are retained-from each occasion when the unit is used a department collection will quickly build up.

KEY SKILLS

(S&L) Contribute in discussion

(R) Read poetry

(W) Write poetry

The level of information about techniques given in the unit is appropriate to the key stage as a whole.

PROGRESSION

Look for individual student progression in:

• the ability to read poetry with understanding and to comment critically

• an understanding of poetic techniques and their employment in the student's writing

• the careful presentation of personal writing.

USING THE UNIT

The poems in this unit have one thing in common. They are all about, or inspired by, parts of the body. That is the starting point for the class.

1 Look at faces

This is a simple way into the unit that encourages close observation. This could be set as a quick exercise at the end of a lesson or a homework, before the real work on the unit starts. Alternatively, ask the students to brainstorm about the photos in groups. An extension task and Copymaster 6 are supplied to support this.

2 Reading poems

You need to make the point that it is not really surprising that people should always have used themselves and the people around them as the raw material for poetry. Underline the point that poetry about bodies is often about something else as well. The reading is best done by you, or by using selected readers.

The discussion with a partner may need to be more focused with some classes. Ask different pairs to focus on particular poems to save time and make sure that all poems are covered in the reporting back. This could be followed up by a written appreciation for more able pupils.

3 What is a poem?

This is a difficult area but it needs to be looked at in Year 7. Students come into secondary education with a myriad of ideas about what their poetry should be like and these notions have to be addressed. Very often, this is done by the teacher commending the best examples but that may be unfair to students who are stuck in a writing rut where poems are concerned.

The level and extent of the discussion will clearly relate to the abilities of the class. With more able pupils, leave time for a lengthy reporting back session and ask some challenging questions. How long is a poem? Does it have to rhyme? If it doesn't have to rhyme, then how are prose and poetry different? How much description makes a poem? The idea is to raise some issues and questions in this session. The Tips and Skills boxes support this activity and may provide some answers for pupils.

The information given in the Skills box is detailed for this level but provides a handy reference point for students who find some of these ideas quite difficult to grasp.

Ask the group to find, and bring in, a copy of a photograph or picture for the next exercise.

4 Look at people

This section takes the focus of the unit back to the student and his or her personal writing. A collection of famous faces – magazines are a useful source – will help those who

have forgotten their picture to get started! Take the poem to draft form but don't expect a final version at this stage.

5 Write your own poem

This is the culmination of the unit where students will integrate the poems they have read, their earlier writing and what they have found out about poetry. Using the idea of a large cut-out body shape should encourage students to read each other's work and to pick up ideas from it.

There will probably be some ribald suggestions at this stage but you could make the point that many poems are actually rude or passionate! Use the Tips box to encourage some careful revision of the work and expect neat, final versions.

EXTENDING THE UNIT

 Every face tells a story

With a partner, use Copymaster 6 to study the faces on page 33. Brainstorm as many ideas you can and quickly fill in the chart. Afterwards choose one face and write a poem about what you see in it.

 Look at a poem in more detail

Pick one of the poems from the unit and write your answers to these questions:

(a) What is the poem called and who wrote it?

(b) What impression of the body does it give?

(c) What else does it say about the personality of the person?

(d) What can you say about the language of the poem? Is there any use of comparisons or sound patterning?

 Look at your hand

Trace the outline of your hand onto a sheet of paper and write a poem where every line begins with the phrase, 'This is the hand that...'

Or, write a poem where the words follow the shape of your hand.

 My beautiful face

Look back at the Skills box and the examples in it. Write new examples based on an unblemished – spotless – face with distinctive eyes, eyebrows and mouth.

 The face

Use the outline Copymaster 7 to help you think of some adjectives and comparisons.

Body rhythms
Every face tells a story

Study the photos. Choose one and describe it in detail. Then, write about what kind of life this person might have.

Adjectives that describe this face...

_____

_____

_____

_____

_____

_____

Comparisons
This face is like...

_____

_____

_____

_____

_____

_____

Association
What does this face make you think of?

_____

_____

_____

_____

_____

_____

Body rhythms
Adjectives and comparisons

Use this outline to help you think of adjectives and comparisons that you could use to describe to faces.

Adjectives to describe:	**Comparisons to describe:**
hair	hair
eyebrows	eyebrows
eyes	eyes
eyelashes	eyelashes
nose	nose
mouth	mouth
skin	skin
teeth	teeth

English Solutions   © Longman Group Limited 1995   **Book 1 unit 3**

A day out

AIMS

✔ This unit gives an opportunity to retrieve information from non-literary materials, an important curriculum requirement.

✔ It can be extended into a local area study, linked to PSE or geography.

✔ The unit teaches formal letter writing.

ADDITIONAL RESOURCES

This is a free-standing unit but can be very effectively reworked using local stimulus materials. To do this, you will need a local map, bus/train timetables and leaflets advertising local places of interest.

KEY SKILLS

(S&L) Structure talk for an audience

(S&L) Respond and restructure

(R) Respond to factual and informative texts

(W) Write in non-literary ways – a formal letter

(W) Understand and use standard English

PROGRESSION

Look for individual student progression in:

- the ability to synthesise information from the full range of sources and to modify first ideas;

- an awareness of audience and context in the presentation of the talk and letter.

USING THE UNIT

1 The background

This is a flexible unit. It can either be worked through by individuals where circumstances make that appropriate or presented as a pair or group activity. It can also be used as a preliminary task, before the class undertakes some more detailed work on the local area.

The unit lends itself best to small group work with no more than four students to a group. However you use the unit, emphasise the constraints that apply to the day out as you introduce it to the class and point out the importance of accuracy in timings and costs.

2 Make plans for the day

3 Decide where to go

A copymaster (CM8) of the chart is provided to help students map the timings for their day and there is also a copy of the area map (CM9). Stress the need to revise schedules and plans, rather than to make an instant – and mistaken – decision and then try to work around it.

Groups will need plenty of time for this activity. Suggest that they read the descriptions of the key places to one another before they start.

4 Explain your choice

Make the point that this is a real exercise and that teachers have to justify this use of time and resources to one another. This is an informal talk – perhaps around a committee table – rather than a formal presentation. If you set up the classroom conference style, this will help to give an informal impression and may reassure nervous speakers. Then, other students can pose the questions. Pinpoint some key issues for the group. Is the activity justifiable? Is the amount of time spent travelling acceptable? Is the day good value for money?

5 Write a letter to the parents

This is a style of writing that most pupils are familiar with. It is a useful type of writing to study because there is a defined audience, some clear information to impart and a reply is required.

This is an ideal opportunity to take the students' work to a neat final version especially if word processing facilities are available. Take the chance to talk about page layout, margins, line and paragraph spacing and text effects such as underlining and embold-ening. These are aspects of word processing that are often assumed to be understood but this is not always the case. One way to start is by setting up the page on the computer with a school heading included so that this part of the exercise does not dominate the importance of a clearly conveyed message.

Even without the IT aspect students should still focus on presentation and you should expect the letter to be carefully presented.

Before the writing starts take the group through the Skills box, highlighting the information it provides in terms of their immediate task.

Copymaster 10 supports this exercise.

6 Prepare a talk for the pupils

The juxtaposition of this and the previous exercise should help to underline the importance of audience. Ask the class why it would not be appropriate to read out the letter to parents or part of it at least. Ask them to think about the style of what they want to say – the trick of giving both some friendly advice and some warnings is the challenge for them.

EXTENDING THE UNIT

1 Write about what happened...

Write about what happened on the group's day out. You can do this as either:

(a) a report of the day for the school magazine

(b) an entry in your diary

(c) a story about one group of pupils

(d) a newspaper report written after things go wrong!

If you have worked as a group, each person should choose a different way of writing about the day.

2 Plan another day out

There is probably lots to do and see in the area where you live. Use information about your local area to plan:

Either a day out for your own class

Or a day out for a pensioners' group

Or a day out for a class at a local junior school.

3 Find out more

Write a letter to one of the possible places to visit listed in the book. Ask about whether student reductions are available for a group of 30 pupils on a weekday afternoon.

4 Find out about your own area

Collect together information about transport and places to visit in your own local area. Plan a day out for your class.

A day out
Planning your day

Day planner

Places of interest	Times for visit	Total time	Arrival and departure times		Costs

English Solutions   © Longman Group Limited 1995   **Book 1 unit 4**

A day out
The map

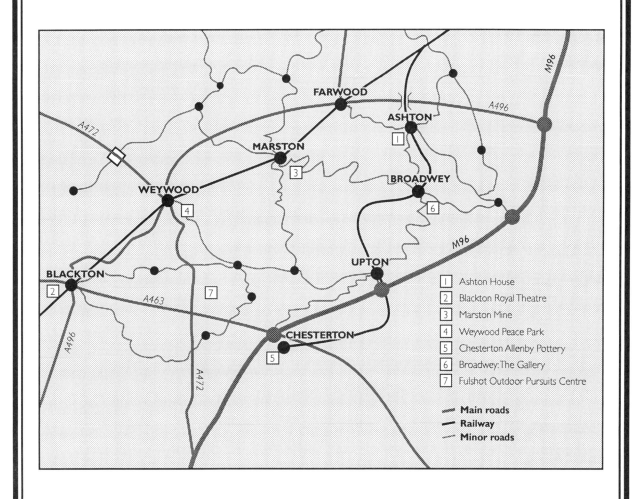

Key:
1 Ashton House
2 Blackton Royal Theatre
3 Marston Mine
4 Weywood Peace Park
5 Chesterton Allenby Pottery
6 Broadwey: The Gallery
7 Fulshot Outdoor Pursuits Centre

— Main roads
— Railway
— Minor roads

English Solutions © Longman Group Limited 1995 **Book 1 unit 4**

A day out
Writing your letter

Use this page blank to help write your letter. Complete it and then write a final neat version.

> Your school name and address
> _____
> _____
> _____
> _____

> today's date
> _____

Dear Parent,

> A reference – like Trip to Theatre for classes in Year 8
> _____

I am writing to give you information about a class outing to

_____

The plan of the day is that we will leave school at

_____

The cost of the trip will be

_____

Please use the tear off slip below to reserve a place

Yours sincerely

> Your name _____
>
> Class teacher _____

It's a small world

AIMS

✔ This unit focuses on the reading of related texts.

✔ It provides some lengthy and detailed passages from literature for study.

✔ The unit offers an opportunity to read some classic texts including some written before 1900.

✔ It encourages a personal response to reading and develops empathic writing skills.

ADDITIONAL RESOURCES

Other stories which contain little people, or a small person's perspective, can be linked to the reading here. One useful example is *Kwaku Ananse and the Greedy Lion* (Andre Deutsch, 1989).

KEY SKILLS

(R) Read narrative – including extracts written before 1900

(W) Write narrative – empathic stories

This unit allows engagement with pre-twentieth century texts, an important element in the new curriculum.

PROGRESSION

Look for individual student progression in:

- the ability to read aloud to a group with confidence and expression

- an understanding of how texts can be compared and contrasted

- the confidence to make inferences about meaning and significance in commenting about the extracts

- the ability to write empathically at the level of style or characterisation.

USING THE UNIT

1 Small in a big world

This extract from *The Little Man*, by Erich Kästner, is intended to give the unit a simple opening. Talk with the class about what it would be like to be so small. The film, *Honey I Shrunk the Kids*, is a promising starting point as are some science fiction classics and the television series, *Land of the Giants*.

Writing or discussion can follow the reading and the latter could be either in pairs or class-based.

2 Big in a small world

Gulliver's Travels will require some intro-duction and support but is a recommended text at this key stage. The extract is visual and many students will have seen the cartoon versions.

The discussion that follows is more focused. The reporting back should be given plenty of time to make sure that all the class are involved.

3 Facing dangers in the big world

These three extracts offer a range of reading to the class at varying levels of difficulty. They can be used to present differentiated tasks to the group using Copymaster 11. Alternatively, ask different groups to prepare readings of one of them for the class.

The task that follows can be varied according to the abilities of the group. The questions can be discussed rather than written for students who have struggled with the extracts. The questions in the Tips box can be used to make the writing more formal for able students.

4 Continue the story

This focus on empathic writing introduces a way of writing about reading that may be new to many students. Talk the group through the Skills box, emphasising that there is more to this kind of writing than merely noting names and places. Illustrate the points by referring to the extracts.

31

It's a small world

Draw the group's attention to the writing model they encountered in How it all Began and ask them to follow the same process of drafting and rewriting. This kind of writing can benefit from peer group comment so suggest that the editing phase of the writing should be shared with a partner.

It is possible to look more closely at the punctuation of direct speech when these stories are edited.

5 Read your stories

Reading the best stories back to the class will help to underline how good empathic writing uses textual hints and allusions to aspects of character to create the atmosphere of an original.

EXTENDING THE UNIT

1 That shrinking feeling...

Imagine that you wake up one day to find that you are only six inches tall. Write about what happens.

2 Read some more about Gulliver

Find a copy of *Gulliver's Travels* and read about his experiences in the land of the giants, Brobdingnag. Report back to the class.

3 Illustrate a scene

Draw one or two pictures that could accompany a new edition of any one of the books from which the extracts in the unit are taken.

4 Writing about yourself

Can you remember when you were too small to do certain things, or when tiny gardens looked like wide open spaces? Write about what you remember of being small. You could write a poem.

5 Write a story

Most of the small people in this unit are male. The women that there are just seem to get into trouble! Invent a race of small people where the women are the leading characters and write a story about their world.

IT'S A small WORLD

THE BORROWERS AFLOAT

Write your answers to these questions:

(a) What happens in the extract you have read?

(b) What do you find out about the three borrowers in the story? What are their names and what are they like?

(c) How many things can you find in the story that tell the reader something about the borrowers' size?

TRUCKERS

Write your answers to these questions:

(a) What happens in the extract you have read?

(b) What does the story tell you about the nomes? What can you say about them generally and what can you say about the different members of this group?

(c) What do you think the nomes are trying to do in this story? Can you suggest a reason why?

(d) What do you think the Thing could be? Why might it be so important?

THE LORD OF THE RINGS

Write your answers to these questions:

(a) What happens in the extract you have read?

(b) What have you found out about the hobbits? What are their names? How do their characters differ?

(c) What makes the black riders frightening?

(d) What do you think the Ring could be? Why might it be so important?

School dinners

AIMS

✔ This unit encourages different forms of writing based on a straightforward and accessible issue.

✔ It offers opportunities for the detailed study of non-literary materials.

✔ It introduces questionnaire and survey skills.

✔ It distinguishes between the writing requirements of letters, leaflets and posters.

✔ There are opportunities to link with aspects of food technology.

ADDITIONAL RESOURCES

Access to other people and their memories about school meals in the past will help. The survey needs time and groups of people who can be asked questions by the group.

KEY SKILLS

(S&L) Listen carefully and positively – carry out a survey

(R) Respond to factual and informative texts – magazine articles

(W) Write in non-literary ways – letters, posters and leaflets

PROGRESSION

Look for individual student progression in:

- the ability to undertake individual research and report back;

- understanding of how surveys work and need to be structured;

- the ability to write reports, leaflets and posters with an understanding of function and audience.

USING THE UNIT

1 Find out about school meals in the past

This first discussion is designed to give the unit its focus. The actual date when free school means ended for secondary pupils is unclear. Many local authorities continued to supply meals, although they were not required to, and carried on with different rates of subsidies. For this reason, it is easier to ask the pupils to find out about meals before 1970, or thereabouts.

Written notes can be combined by groups into a single report or compared in a class discussion. Some pupils may like to try a video or audiotape interview with an older person. If that is likely, role play the interview with the group beforehand.

2 Find out about school meals today

3 Check your reading

This magazine article takes a strident line on school dinners and should open up some lively discussion. The questions for discussion leave space deliberately for students to take issue with what is said.

Some groups will benefit from a class reading.

4 A survey – are your friends healthy eaters?

Designing a questionnaire is a sophisticated skill. This can be either an individual or a small group task. With most classes, groups of two or three are probably best. Copymaster 13 offers a simple prepared survey sheet for less able pupils or you could modify Copymaster 2 from Unit 1, My top ten.

Encourage groups to think about what a sample is and how complex the notion of a representative sample can be. Ask the class to think about why the class itself probably does not provide a representative sample of schoolchildren in the UK. Answers should include age, background, race and so on.

Remember to give warnings about where students go and who they talk to if the survey is carried out off school premises. These are reinforced by the Tips box.

There may be opportunities to lay out the survey sheets using DTP facilities.

5 Prepare your report

With some groups, you will want to introduce two key terms at this stage. Survey data has to be analysed and then interpreted and it can be interesting to separate the two. Ask individuals or groups to analyse their findings and report two findings to the class. Discuss whether these have any significance.

The report for the school magazine is a challenging task for the students but, with careful preparation, it will be done well. Encourage the use of graphics and talk about how, for example, the pie charts can be 'pies' and the bars, 'chips' in order to lighten the presentation.

Finding an audience for the finished writing, such as a year assembly, will be well worthwhile.

6 Persuade people to eat healthier foods

The additional material that is provided here is intended to support this task. Purpose, audience and form are difficult concepts, here approached at quite a low level. As you go round the class, ask individuals to tell you how they were aware of the impact of their finished work as it was written.

The final session, where the work is displayed, is a chance to discuss these features of writing by pointing to good examples.

EXTENDING THE UNIT

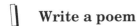

1 Write a poem

Write a poem about school dinners in the past. Make it as descriptive – and as nasty – as you can.

2 Give your own views

Do you agree with the views that the articles express? Do all school children exist on unhealthy diets? Or, do you think the articles are not being fair? Discuss your own ideas about a healthy diet with your partner. Make notes on your discussion under the following headings.

A healthy diet consists of … An unhealthy diet consists of …

Report back to the class.

3 Find out more

Ask your technology teacher to help you find out more about healthy eating or carry out some research in the library. Find out what makes some foods healthy or unhealthy and report back to the class.

Find out what you can about the eating disorders that teenagers can suffer from. Find out about bulimia and anorexia. Report back to the class.

4 Design a menu

What would your ideal school dinner menu consist of? Design a series of menus for a week that you think would be tasty, healthy and cheap.

5 Eat better and help others

Organise a healthy bread and cheese lunch one day in aid of a famine relief charity.

School dinners

The healthy things that pupils should eat	The unhealthy things that pupils eat

School dinners

Are your friends healthy eaters?

Use this sheet to find out whether ten of your friends are healthy eaters. First read through these questions. Then ask your friends for their answers.

QUESTION	A	B	C
1 How many packets of crisps or snacks do you eat a day?	Three or more	One	None usually
2 Do you eat chocolate?	Every day	Once or twice a week	Less than once a week
3 Do you eat breakfast cereals?	Every day	Once or twice a week	Less than once a week
4 What kind of cooked potato do you eat most often?	Chips	Boiled or mashed	Cooked in its skin
5 How would you describe the way you eat?	Unhealthy	Average	Healthy

Now use this chart to record the results. Put in the names of the people you ask and their answers – A, B or C. If they are not sure, ask them to choose the closest answer.

NAME	Q1	Q2	Q3	Q4	Q5
1					
2					
3					
4					
5					
6					
7					
8					
9					
10					

Now answer these questions:
1 How many of your friends have cereals at least once a week?
2 What percentage of your friends have chips every day?
3 Who eats more chocolate – boys or girls?
4 What percentage have chips and chocolate or a snack every day?
5 Are your friends more healthy than you expected or more unhealthy? Has your survey helped you answer this question?

Dear diary

AIMS

✔ This unit encourages the reading and writing of diaries. It is ideal for the start of a new year.

✔ It introduces the study of a diary as a form of writing.

✔ It provides opportunities for the discussion of current events and for links with history.

✔ The unit supports personal diary writing by the student.

ADDITIONAL RESOURCES

An anthology of extracts from famous diaries will support the work in this unit. Many of the students are likely to be interested in reading the complete diaries of Zlata Filipović and Anne Frank. Other up-to-date information about the war in Yugoslavia will be helpful.

KEY SKILLS

(S&L) Reach conclusions through discussion

(R) Respond to factual and informative texts

(W) Write narrative

(W) Write in non-literary ways

PROGRESSION

Look for individual student progression in:

• the ability to respond sensitively to what is read

• an understanding of how a writer feels and reacts to real events

• the capacity to express personal feelings.

USING THE UNIT

1 Zlata's diary

This unit is ideal for the start of a new year and one way to start is to talk generally about diaries. Pose these questions for class or group discussion:

• Do any of you keep a diary? What kind of things do you write in it?

• Is it intended for other people to read (either now, or in the future), or is it a private place to write things just for yourself?

• Have any of you read a published diary written by someone famous? Do you know of anyone who has had their diary published?

• Do girls keep diaries more often than boys? Why?

• When you write in a diary, how is the style of writing different from writing a story or an essay?

Zlata Filopović's diary was a publishing sensation for understandable reasons. It is a powerful and well written text with a very personal view of what it is like to be caught up in a bloody civil war. It is especially interesting because students see this war as television images where people die and starve at a distance. The diary underlines the fact that the person on the television is only a thousand miles away. Also, Zlata is a typical teenager. She has the same interests and aspirations as her equivalent in an English classroom. It is important to try to get this feeling over to the class.

The reading of the extracts from Zlata's diary is best done as pairs or singly. The discussion may need more focus with some students. Ask them to list her friends and family and to summarise the events she describes.

The letter exercise is a chance to write personally about the reading. If you think the class is unlikely to respond to this, you could ask them to write about some of the events described as if they were one of Zlata's friends.

2 Writing as if you were there

Anne Frank's diary provides a contrast to Zlata's. Anne – a few years older – is more philosophical about events and, perhaps, a little more detached. However, what she writes about is even more horrific. Encourage the class to take all this into account as they compare the two writers.

The next exercise can be a major piece of writing linked to current work in history. Alternatively, contemporary events may give it an immediate focus. In either circumstance, encourage some careful research beforehand.

Emphasise the idea that this is a diary and talk through the Tips box with the group. Note how the task allows you to talk about the features of diary writing without opening up personal diaries to comment.

3 Writing your own diary

An excellent time to use this unit is at the start of the Spring term when the new year makes people think of diaries. Diaries are private documents, so the notion of preparing the diary for publication is necessary and should work well in the classroom. Make the distinction clear. Reference to recently published diaries may help if any are currently in the public gaze.

One way to underline the change in audience is to say that the published diary is to appear in a national newspaper and to set it out in that way.

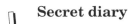

EXTENDING THE UNIT

1 Secret diary

Anne Frank could have been killed just for keeping her diary. Imagine that your country has been invaded by foreign powers, or there has been a violent revolution, or invaders have come from outer space. Write a secret diary to describe what has really happened for future generations.

2 Read more...

Find the full version of Zlata's diary and read it. Write about the character of Zlata as it is revealed in the complete book and about two of the most moving events in her story.

3 Adapt the story

How would you turn part of Zlata's story into a radio programme? Work as a small group to present one or more of the extracts as it might be used on radio. Use voices and sound effects to make the programme as lively and exciting as you can.

4 Read other diaries

Many famous people keep diaries and often publish them. Find – and read – the diary of someone you admire. Report back to the class.

5 Meet a star

Magazines often have diaries in them. Imagine that you have won the trip of a lifetime to meet one of your favourite stars in an exciting place. Write the diary of your three-day trip.

6 Writing with power

Write the diary entries that you might have written on the two or three days surrounding a momentous or memorable event in your own life.

Early writing

AIMS

✔ This unit explores the history of writing, developing the student's knowledge about language.

✔ It uses pictograms to make links between the present and the past.

✔ The unit is designed as a spring-board for further independent research into language.

ADDITIONAL RESOURCES

There are some excellent reference materials available on early writing which can be used to extend the range of the unit.

KEY SKILLS

(S&L) Understand the development of language

(R) Engage with content and language

(W) Write in non-literary ways

(W) Use presentational devices

PROGRESSION

Look for individual student progression in:

• the ability to see language as a system or code

• the capacity to undertake independent research.

USING THE UNIT

1 The importance of speech

After the group discussions, ask the class to look back at the short extract about the Algonkin Indians. Ask them to talk about how modern society is replacing writing. Why do people read fewer books today? Why are talking books so popular? What are the advantages of video books? How do people send one another notes in business? How can video evidence replace written evidence in court rooms?

Then, talk about the advantages of writing for primitive people. What did the medium enable? Trade? The accurate transmission of messages over distances? Laws? The development of stories and history?

The conclusions might be that, once invented, writing was certain to develop as quickly and as inevitably as video recorders have. Bulky cumbersome models give way to simpler variations and a wider choice.

This could lead to a homework on the value of writing.

2 Using pictures in writing

Sumerian pictograms were a starting point for writing. Most pupils will enjoy these tasks.

3 Adding sounds to writing

Conceptually, this is a difficult leap. However, the video recorder analogy works. Pictogram languages, like early video recorders, were slow and lacked detail, while hieroglyphics were faster and allowed generalisation.

The most important development was the realisation that pictograms could be used to represent sounds rather than objects. For instance, the symbol for an arrow 'ti' was used to write 'life', for which the word was also 'ti'. This meant that when the Akkadians, who spoke a completely differ-ent language from the Sumerians, came to be the dominant power in Mesopotamia shortly after 2000 BC, the Akkadians were able to adopt the cuneiform script to write their own language.

The writing system developed by the Egyptians consisted of three kinds of sign:

- pictograms – stylised drawings
- phonograms – used to represent sounds
- determinants – used to show which kind of object or being was being written about.

Interestingly, the use of phonograms means that the sounds of the ancient Egyptian language can be partially recovered. That is, of course, impossible with pictograms.

It is worth noting how, at this time, the technology of writing was lagging behind the ideas. Carving on stone or printing on clay must have been a very slow process! Egyptian scribes therefore invented a different script, known as hieratic, which used the same elements as hieroglyphics but in a much more flowing form. All this underlines the sense that this was a technology in the making.

4 Using an alphabet

An alphabet is a sound-based system. The principle is that words are broken down into common sounds which can be re-combined in many ways. Try to emphasise the sense of progression in all of this. The pictograms became more and more stylised until they were reduced to one or two strokes. These then became identified with the sounds that made up the words.

The lack of vowels in the Phoenician alphabet is likely to cause some confusion in the messages.

5 Using pictures again

This exercise can be refined and extended with the help of the art teacher. Produce properly finished pieces of design with a commentary alongside explaining what the student was trying to convey and how he or she went about this.

Finish the unit with independent research into some of the issues raised. Class members can find out more about the different systems mentioned in the unit or the lives of the people who used them.

End with a general discussion about the issues. For example, why do we write from left to right? Cuneiform was often arranged in columns and hieroglyphics were usually written from right to left. However, some read downwards and others from left to right. Chinese writing is from right to left. One disc discovered in Crete is inscribed in a spiral pattern and would have been read by turning the disc.

EXTENDING THE UNIT

1 **Life without writing**

As a class, divide into three sets of groups: A, B and C.

The people in the A groups should put away all their pens and other writing equipment.

The people in the B groups can make written notes of their discussions.

The people in the C groups can make notes of their discussions in any form that does not involve writing.

Then, your first task is to talk about how life today would be different if writing didn't exist. What things wouldn't exist? What would school be like? Would our present society be possible?

One person in each group should be prepared to report its findings back to the whole class. As each group reports back, compare the different ways that the speakers organised their reports. Which worked best? Which groups had the most difficult task? What methods did the C groups use to make their notes?

2 **Go Phoenician**

Write a note to a friend. Then, write it out again without any vowels (a, e, i, o and u). What parts of it are easy to read? Which words are most difficult?

3 **Modern pictograms**

Collect as many of these as you can find. The Highway Code will be a good place to start! You may also find them used in advertising and in business letterheads and logos.

4 **Research into language**

Use your local library to find out more about the people who used hieroglyphics. In what other ways did they develop new technologies? Write up your findings as a short project.

5 **Research into alphabets**

Make a collection of as many alphabets and writing systems as you can. If there is someone in your class who uses, for instance, Cyrillic or Quôc-ngu ask them to write out a sample and explain how it is written and used. Ask at your local library for leaflets written in different scripts. When you have made your collection, try to locate where the alphabets and scripts you have found are mainly used on a map of the world.

Early writing
Language detectives

Study these five different scripts. Use your researching skills to identify as many of them as you can. Books in libraries and foreign newspapers will help you. Ask friends as well.

既然必须和新的群众的时代相结合，就必须彻底解决个人和群众的关系问题。鲁迅的两句诗，"横眉冷对千夫指，俯首甘为孺子牛"，应该成为我们的座右铭。"千夫"在这里就是说敌人，对于无论什么凶恶的敌人我们决不屈服。"孺子"在这里就是说无产阶级和人民大众。一切共产党员，一切革命家，一切革命的文

Κι ὁ νοῦς του ἀγκάλιασε πονετικὰ τὴν Κρήτη. Τὴν ἀγαποῦσε σὰν ἕνα πράμα ζωντανό, ζεστό, ποὺ 'χε στόμα καὶ φώναζε, καὶ μάτια κι ἔκλαιγε, καὶ δὲν ἦταν καμωμένη ἀπὸ πέτρες καὶ χώματα κι ἀπὸ ρίζες δεντρῶν, παρὰ ἀπὸ χιλιάδες χιλιάδες παπποῦδες καὶ μάνες, ποὺ δὲν πεθαίνουν ποτέ τους, παρὰ ζοῦν καὶ μαζεύουνται κάθε Κυριακὴ στὶς ἐκκλησιὲς κι ἀγριεύουν κάθε τόσο, ξετυλίγουν μέσα

માનવીના હૈયાને નંદવામાં વાર શી ?
અધબોલ્યા   બોલડે,
થાડે   અબોલડે,
પાચાશા હૈયાને પીજવામાં વાર શી ?

וְהָיָה ׀ בְּאַחֲרִית הַיָּמִים נָכוֹן יִהְיֶה הַר בֵּית־יְהוָה בְּרֹאשׁ הֶהָרִים וְנִשָּׂא מִגְּבָעוֹת וְנָהֲרוּ אֵלָיו כָּל־הַגּוֹיִם: וְהָלְכוּ עַמִּים רַבִּים וְאָמְרוּ לְכוּ ׀ וְנַעֲלֶה אֶל־הַר־יְהוָה אֶל־בֵּית אֱלֹהֵי יַעֲקֹב וְיֹרֵנוּ מִדְּרָכָיו וְנֵלְכָה בְּאֹרְחֹתָיו כִּי מִצִּיּוֹן

«Что это? я падаю? у меня ноги подкашиваются», подумал он и упал на спину. Он раскрыл глаза, надеясь увидать, чем кончилась борьба французов с артиллеристами, и желая знать, убит или нет рыжий артиллерист, взяты или спасены пушки. Но он ничего не видал. Над ним не было ничего уже,

The tomb of the last Pharaoh

AIMS

✔ This unit develops writing skills across a range of writing types.

✔ It allows the features of different writing types to be compared.

✔ The adventure format encourages all students.

✔ There are opportunities to extend the unit in other directions.

ADDITIONAL RESOURCES

Adventure game books, information on explorers and treasure hunters or a viewing of the film *Raiders of the Lost Ark* would all add to the effect of this unit. Also, there are more materials available now about the many women explorers who have gone largely unnoticed by history.

KEY SKILLS

(S&L) Reach conclusions through discussion

(R) Respond to factual and informative texts

(W) Write narrative

(W) Write in non-literary ways

PROGRESSION

Look for individual student progression in:

• the ability to take a shaping role in the group discussions

• an understanding of the demands made by the different writing types appearing in this unit.

USING THE UNIT

1 Making a start

Some of the group will already know how to play adventure games through the books written by writers like Steve Jackson and Ian Livingstone. Others will have played similar board games or games on computers. With the class – or in small groups – discuss what previous experience the members of the class have of playing adventure games. Pose these questions:

• Which games have you played?

• How do you play them?

• Are any of you playing an adventure game for the first time?

• Are adventure games more popular with girls or boys? Why do you think this is?

• What makes an adventure game exciting? The setting? The task? The journey? The prize?

Lead the discussion into the search for Tutankhamen's treasure and read Howard Carter's account with the group. The task that follows could be written after some preliminary discussion.

2 The quest begins

Episode 1: From this point onwards the class needs to work in groups. However, the unit is flexible in letting you decide how far to support the students. The journal that starts here is a key part of the unit. It should be seen as a collection of documents rather than as a diary. So, describing a character and drawing the map should allow a sense of authenticity to be created. Emphasise the need to create a 'real' person with a past and a personality. This could be done, for example, with a collection of press-cuttings and other documents.

Episode 2: TALK. This is a well-known model for oral discussion. Focus it by pointing out that what the group decides on may have an important bearing on the success of the quest.

Episode 3: LETTER WRITING. The letter writing can be supported with discussion. Stress that this is to be an informal – but informative – letter evoking the place for people without access to film and television. Raise the issue of audience and stress paragraphing and layout.

Episode 4: IMPROVISATION. Ask groups to prepare their improvisations and then show them to the class. Highlight those where people act in character and respond to the information on the page.

Episode 5: DESCRIPTION. The description of the valley should make full use of adjectival description, comparison and a colourful vocabulary. Stress these in redrafting the work.

Episode 6: NARRATIVE. Discuss the use of the present historic before the exercise starts and the effect of using short sentences.

Help the class by asking them to imagine themselves in the situation with a portable tape recorder.

SCRIPT. Able pupils should be able to see how the script differs from the first-person narrative. Revise the script layout with the group if necessary. Act out the finished scripts.

Episode 7: NARRATIVE CLIMAX. Encourage the group to see this as the ending of the quest and refer them back to Carter's account as a possible model.

Afterword: NEWSPAPER ARTICLE / FORMAL LETTER WRITING. The two options here complete the unit and create time for slower workers to catch up. Show the group how it is possible to bring all their 'documents' together to create a picture of the journey through a collection of realia.

EXTENDING THE UNIT

1 **Write another story**

Write the further adventures of the hero you have invented for this unit, beginning with the discovery of a clue to a new treasure.

2 **Write your own adventure game**

Use Copymaster 15 to write an adventure game based on the story you have told.

3 **Research**

Find out as much as you can about the discovery of Tutankhamen's treasure and the curse that was said to have followed the explorers.

The tomb of the last Pharaoh
Write your own adventure

An adventure game story is like a tree. The things that happen on each page offer the reader two choices and each choice is like a branch. The stories can quickly become very complicated but the trick is to make them go round in circles or to arrive, by different routes, at the same page. Use this page to plan a simple story, then try a more complicated one of your own. Make some choices lead back to earlier pages or end in death! Otherwise you will have too many pages. Try to end up with the chance of a happy ending for some of the people who play your game.

START HERE

PAGE 1
Describe the event which starts your story. Perhaps you are out somewhere when something suddenly happens to you. You could react in two ways. If you choose the first, go to page 2. If you choose the second, go to page 3.

PAGE 2
This was the wrong choice! (Perhaps it puts you in danger.) There are two ways to escape. If you choose the first, go to page 4. If you choose the second, go to page 5.

PAGE 3
This choice was the better one. Describe what happens and give yourself two possible ways to move on. If you choose the first, go to page 6. If you choose the second, go to page 7.

PAGE 4
Write a further page of the story with two outcomes. If you choose the first one, you come to a gory end! If you choose the second, go to page 5.

PAGE 5
Your story continues and there are two ways out of this page. If you choose the first, go on to page 8. If you choose the second, go back to page 3.

PAGE 6
Another exciting event with two possible outcomes. If you take the first, go on to page 8. If you choose the second, go to page 9.

PAGE 7
This page ends with giving you two ways forward in your adventure. If you choose the first one, you come to a terrifying end. If you choose the second, you are out of the game but you live to play again.

PAGE 8
There is no way out! Your game is over.

PAGE 9
You have won!

English Solutions   © Longman Group Limited 1995   **Book 1 unit 9**

Turned on its head

AIMS

✔ This unit explores how one form of comic writing works.

✔ It shows how comedy can carry a serious message.

✔ It presents lengthy extracts from two short plays.

✔ It provides a model for the presentation of playscripts.

ADDITIONAL RESOURCES

Other materials relating to Robin Hood – the television series, films and stories – will be useful as will a selection of comic writing and television clips.

KEY SKILLS

(R) Engage with content and language

(R) Read plays

(W) Write script

PROGRESSION

Look for individual student progression in:

• a clear understanding of what the writers of the plays are trying to achieve

• the ability to select and identify key scenes or techniques

• competence and confidence in the writing and presentation of playscripts.

USING THE UNIT

1 Act out a scene

Most students will know this play from television, where the series proved very popular and has been repeated. They are also likely to be familiar with the story of Robin Hood, courtesy of the Kevin Costner film. Finally, this first discussion can build on what the

class already knows about creation stories and myths from the first unit in book 1, *How it all began*.

It will be interesting to find out what the students know. Ask them to vote on whether or not Robin was a real person, for example. The evidence for this is thin but the character is referred to in *Piers Plowman* and other early ballads.

If he had lived, then it would have been between 1150 and 1200. He may have been born at Locksley in Nottingham – the character's name is Locksley in Sir Walter Scott's *Ivanhoe*.

The evidence for Maid Marian and Little John is even more limited but the appeal of the pastoral idyll and the idea of robbing the rich to feed the poor retains a universal appeal. In this sense, one could make the point that the ballads about Robin were highly subversive in their time – they were like medieval equivalents of Viz!

The extracts can be read or acted out. In particular, the first extract, set on the bridge, lends itself to a dramatic presentation. Point out for the class the need to ham up the playing, or the reading, for comic effect. Discuss how the voice of the narrator could be played in different ways – deadpan, football commentator, news reporter.

If follow up work is required, ask the class to write another episode from the story of Robin Hood – the first meeting with the large Friar Truck, the Italian monk, Friar Eggs or the historically disempowered Sister Tuck might work well!

2 What makes a scene funny?

The notion of role reversal for comic effect is quite difficult. In this playscript it is achieved by changing names, turning events around and playing jokes with language. Completing the chart in Copymaster 16 should bring these ideas into the open.

3 Reading *Bill's New Frock*

These extracts take the notion of turning a scene on its head a stage further. This is a much more subtle play and the questions bring out some of the deeper messages. The answers can be written up after some preliminary discussion.

Bill's New Frock raises another issue as it has been criticised for reinforcing negative images of girls. In this reading, Bill is horrified at being a girl because of all the stupid things that girls do, so the – ultimate – joke is at the expense of female lives. The writer, Anne Fine, would strenuously resist attempts to read the play in this way but it is an interesting area for discussion.

4 Write your own script

Starting on the right track is the key to success here. Talk the class through the steps for success and encourage redrafting from the start. If the ideas don't flow, suggest some of the ideas given here as a starting point. Classic tales are another good source. Suggest a scene from Malice in Wonderland about a nasty little girl who likes to chase rabbits or the story of the Stupid Six who solve crimes more slowly than do Enid Blyton's characters!

The Tips box supports presentation in some detail and is worth reinforcing. The idea that a scene takes place in 'real' time and space is one that often goes unnoticed in script writing. There are obvious opportunities for word processing here – perhaps to produce a more permanent collection of the best scripts.

Acting out a scene is the true test of its worth. If possible, videotape two or three of them and discuss exactly where the humour is and how it could be developed.

EXTENDING THE UNIT

1 Read more...

Find the full version of *Maid Marian and her Merry Men* or *Bill's New Frock*. Read the play and report back to the class on what else happened and what you thought of it.

2 Research

See what else you can find out about the legend of Robin Hood from the encyclopedias in your school and local libraries.

3 Sharon's New Shorts

Try a plot somersault! Write a story, or playscript, called Sharon's New Shorts about a girl who turns into a boy and what happens to her when she gets to school.

4 Act it out

Choose one of the extracts from the unit and present it to a year assembly. Explain to the group what the message of the play is.

5 Adaptation

Rewrite the first extract from *Maid Marian and her Merry Men* as it could appear in a book version for primary school pupils. You will need to add a description of the setting and the background to the story, as well as describing what the characters do and how they speak.

6 Watch a movie

Watch the film *Mrs Doubtfire*. The screenplay was written by Anne Fine who also wrote *Bill's New Frock*. Discuss how the film and the story are similar in some ways and very different in others.

Turned on its head
What makes a scene funny?

	What there is in the play	What you would expect
Names		
Events		
What people do		
What people say		

Getting into print

AIMS

✔ This unit explores the effects of changing the shape and size of the print on a page.

✔ It introduces students to the terms they will encounter in word processing and desktop publishing.

✔ The unit foregrounds the presentation of written work in an interesting and unusual way.

ADDITIONAL RESOURCES

The unit should be supported by large quantities of printed material – magazines, newsletters, advertising leaflets and, if possible, posters. Part of the introduction to the unit can involve finding these materials. Access to computers with word processing and desktop publishing facilities will be invaluable in exploring the potential of the unit. David Crystal's *Cambridge Encyclopaedia of Language* (CUP, 1987) also contains a wealth of fascinating information on this subject.

KEY SKILLS

(S&L) Contribute in discussion

(R) Respond to factual and informative texts

(W) Write in non-literary ways

(W) Use presentational devices

PROGRESSION

Look for individual student progression in:

• a consideration of the relationship between text and layout and the impact of text effects

• competence in using word processing and desktop publishing facilities

• the ability to visualise a layout and to complete it accordingly.

USING THE UNIT

1 Choosing a typeface

Start by looking at the examples shown in the book but lead on quickly to wider discussion and student research. Start with typefaces and fonts. There seems to be no consensus over the terminology and they are now sometimes called character sets as well. You might point out to the class that we have come to where we are now through a three stage development. It is sometimes forgotten that before printing was widely available, calligraphy (the art of handwriting) had already defined different ways of writing in great detail.

The invention of modern printing in the fifteenth century was based on the use of moveable metal type. Since then it is estimated that around 10,000 typefaces have been designed. Most of the time we take typefaces for granted; suggest that students take a closer look at street nameplates and traffic route signs on their way home to see two of the most famous modern typefaces.

The typewriter may be mentioned in discussion but was limited to only one typeface through most of its history. However, it has left us with the QWERTY keyboard. This keyboard was said to have been designed to keep the most used keys apart and prevent them from jamming in rapid use but it is more likely that the design was a historical accident. It has even been suggested that the top line contained the letters of the word 'typewriter' to help salesmen demonstrate the invention to customers! Although most people are right-handed, the left hand does 56% of the work on a typewriter and many of the most common letter links use only one hand. Type the word 'addressed' as an example!

The third change has been the use of electronics in publishing which has gradually made metal type superfluous. It has made fonts very much cheaper – they no longer have to be made in metal – and to be changed in very minor ways. There are now hundreds of modified versions of typical typefaces, all with different names.

Electronics has had another influence on typefaces. The traditional typeface box, or printers fount, has 275 characters including lower case, capitals, italics, fractions, accents, commercial symbols and so on. Electronic text – as used on Prestel or Ceefax – often makes do with only 96. Dot-matrix text of the kind used on many computer printers and public information systems makes all of its characters fit in a 12×10 matrix: – this is why the tail on the letter 'g' is often squashed on these printers.

The session should end with a wider discussion of typefaces. The typical school library should provide plenty of examples.

2 Deciding on a size

This section highlights, through a study of only one variable, the importance of audience. The message here is that designers and printers think hard about what they want their choice of point sizes and typefaces to say to the reader.

3 Using font and size for effect

The discussion of the newsletters should raise other issues apart from the choice of font and its size. Talk the group through the way that columns, boxes and white space can be used on a page for extra effect. Show how, as in Lewis Carroll's poem, a picture can be created. The poems here are probably best hand-written. A long acquaintance with computers is required to create images of this sort and unless plenty of time is available the use of technology will probably have to end in compromise!

4 Design your own newsletter

5 Publishing your newsletter

The time spent on these tasks will necessarily relate to the technology available. The Tips box and the task allow the design to be completed either on paper or screen but the latter is probably preferable in the context of this unit. It will also allow the publishing to be more authentic. That said, the lessons of layout and design can be understood from a paste-up version of the newsletter page. One useful trick can be to produce the newsletter at A3 size and then reduce it to A4 for publication, giving an extra neatness to the final version.

EXTENDING THE UNIT

1 Finding more fonts

Use Copymaster 17 to find and record other examples of fonts. Look in newspapers, advertising leaflets and magazines for your examples. Stick your examples on to the page.

2 Playing with printers

Even the most advanced computer printers use dots to make up an image of the letters they will print. The simplest printers may use as few as nine dots per letter so that the letters appear to be broken up. However, many printers now found in schools use over 300 dots per inch and it is then very difficult to see individual dots at all. Find out about and collect an example of:

- a 9 or 24 pin dot matrix print out
- a dot matrix NLQ (near letter quality) print out
- a laser printer document.

Report back to the class saying where you found each example, and compare them.

3 The days before computers...

Look back at some of the earlier writing technologies before computing. Find out all you can about one of the following topics:

- The illuminated manuscripts produced by medieval monks
- William Caxton and the birth of printing
- The history of handwriting – calligraphy.

Report back to the class or write a short topic report.

Getting into print
Finding more fonts

Stick examples of the different fonts you find in your research in the correct columns.

Serif fonts	Sans-serif fonts	Decorative fonts

A day in your life

AIMS

- ✔ This unit is designed for the start of a school year.
- ✔ It encourages students to talk and write about themselves.
- ✔ It introduces autobiographical writing within a simple framework.

ADDITIONAL RESOURCES

Other autobiographical materials will be useful. Copies of similar articles from the *Sunday Times* will also extend the unit.

KEY SKILLS

(S&L) Contribute in discussion

(R) Engage with content and language

(W) Write narrative

PROGRESSION

Look for individual student progression in:

- the ability to stand back and make observations about personal events
- competence in the shaping of writing
- an awareness of form and audience in the magazine article.

USING THE UNIT

1 One way to write an autobiography

The use of the *Sunday Times* model for this writing is intended to give it structure and a sense of audience. Open the subject by asking who in the group has kept a diary. Point out that people would not like their diaries to be read but that autobiography is written for an audience. The sense of 'putting the record straight' and 'telling it as it was' is an important thread in this kind of writing.

At the beginning of a new year, ask partners to read the articles to one another and to begin the discussion before joining with other pairs to make groups of four. At this point introduce the Skills box and talk the class through the ideas it presents about reading magazines as a preliminary to the writing of their own articles.

With some classes, it would be possible to follow up the discussion with some written work. More able children can write a commentary on the two articles under the headings of Content, Layout and Style. For less confident writers, Copymaster 18 and the 'Extending the unit' section (Task 1) offer alternatives.

2 A day in your own life

The steps for success structure this task and provide a chance for pupils at the start of the year to revisit and reinforce good practice. Presentation is important and should be emphasised. This is a unit that will benefit from the use of word processing and DTP facilities if these are available.

EXTENDING THE UNIT

1 Meet Ganesh or Neneh

Imagine that you are a journalist and have been invited to meet either Ganesh Sittampalam or Neneh Cherry. Using what you can find out about them from the articles, write an account of your meeting.

2 Find a pen-pal

Write a letter about yourself – based on your article – to a new pen-friend in a foreign country.

3 Other ways of writing about yourself

These articles are one form of autobiography or writing about yourself. Find as many examples of other ways that people write about themselves in magazines. Look out for questionnaires, answers to readers' questions and accounts of particular events.

4 Read an autobiography

Find and read the autobiography of a famous person who you admire. Report back to the class on what you have read.

A day in your life
Looking closer

Read the articles about Ganesh Sittampalam and Neneh Cherry. Then, decide whether these statements are true or false. Put a tick in the correct column.

STATEMENTS ABOUT GANESH

		True	False
1	Ganesh has to leave the house at 7.30 to catch his train.	☐	☐
2	Ganesh doesn't like school very much – or at least not every subject.	☐	☐
3	When he did his maths degree he was a full-time student at university.	☐	☐
4	He is always in a hurry to get home and finish his homework.	☐	☐
5	Ganesh has a computer that he uses only for schoolwork.	☐	☐

STATEMENTS ABOUT NENEH

		True	False
1	Neneh finds it easy to write the lyrics for songs.	☐	☐
2	She likes cooking.	☐	☐
3	Michael Stipe of REM is one of her heroes.	☐	☐
4	Tyson and Pajah are her children.	☐	☐
5	Neneh does not like being told what to wear.	☐	☐

A day in your life
Reading the articles

At first glance, you might think that Ganesh and Neneh only talk about what they do each day. Look again. To help you, copy and complete the chart below. See how much, and what kind of, information the writers add to the factual accounts of their days.

Time of day	What happens	Other information about:		
		Them and their work	The places where they live and work	Their friends

English Solutions   © Longman Group Limited 1995   **Book 2 unit 1**

Play with a purpose

AIMS

✔ This unit explores plays that convey a serious message.

✔ It encourages students to be aware of ideas and inferences in their reading.

✔ It revisits the writing of playscripts.

ADDITIONAL RESOURCES

The Restaurant at the End of the Universe by Douglas Adams has passages that would be suitable for reading aloud by the teacher. There is also an extract from *Gulliver's Travels* in the unit called It's a small world in *English Solutions* book 1.

KEY SKILLS

(S&L) Structure talk for an audience

(S&L) Respond and restructure

(R) Read plays

(W) Write script

PROGRESSION

Look for individual student progression in:

• the capacity to talk about what is comic and significant in the playscript;

• a willingness to take a lead in performance and to interpret the script;

• the ability to structure and organise the writing of a playscript.

USING THE UNIT

1 Read and act out a scene

Anne Fine's *Celebrity Chicken* is likely to be better known as a short story than as a playscript. It may be worth organising the first reading with the whole class so as to highlight the humour. There should be parts for almost everyone. The full cast for these extracts requires 18 voices:

Cora, the celebrity chicken	Cora
2 Little Green Citizens	LGC 1 and LGC2
4 Chickens	Chickens 1–4
A man	Man
A woman	Woman
A girl	Girl
A boy	Boy
A baby	Baby
4 Little Green Customers	Customers 1–4
Howard Green	Howard
Miss Green Glamore	Miss G

Underline the humour of the extracts – this is not always apparent on a first reading. The discussion that follows is best group-based. One way to approach it is to ask different groups to work on each of the four scenes and then to report back to the class. This will mean that the performance covers all four extracts.

Stress the need to make this performance comic. Talk through the ideas on the page and ask the groups to come up with other ideas of their own.

This section of the unit can be made more important and be taken through to a proper performance – perhaps for a year assembly.

2 Look at the message of the play

Understanding a writer's inferences and the message of a play is quite hard for many students. The important idea is that Anne Fine set out with a purpose in her mind as she started to write this book and play. The questions can be discussed and a written follow-up would be appropriate for students who are coming to grips with the ideas.

The box, Comic writing with a message, takes the ideas of the unit outside this particular text. Experts disagree about exactly what satire is, but television programmes may provide a contemporary model that will guide the writing in the next section of the unit.

3 Write your own play

This is a challenging task and the level of ability in the class will be a guide as to what to expect. One option is to ask the class to take the suggestions in the unit and to work on one or two of them as role-plays before any writing starts. In this way, individuals are less likely to take wrong avenues.

There is a detailed guide to script layout in *English Solutions* book 1 in Unit 11 Turned on its head.

EXTENDING THE UNIT

1 Read more...

Find either the full text of the play, *Celebrity Chicken*, or the story version. Report back to the class on what else happens in either of them.

2 Write another scene

Write a scene from *Celebrity Chicken* explaining how Cora travels from Earth to the Little Green Planet.

3 Look hard at the arguments

From your reading of the extracts answer these questions:

(a) What reasons does the Man give for not being eaten?

(b) What reasons do the Little Green Citizens give for eating people?

(c) How does Cora justify eating grubs?

(d) Why does Cora criticise the Little Green Citizens?

4 Find out more

Find out more about how chickens are reared in sheds and cages. Do you think that Anne Fine is right in her criticism?

Factbooks

AIMS

✔ This unit offers the chance to engage with non-literary texts of a specific kind.

✔ It explores a resource that students are likely to make considerable use of in their daily studies.

✔ The unit looks at the features of information writing.

✔ It gives students the opportunity to present information in writing.

ADDITIONAL RESOURCES

Students will benefit from access to a wide range of information books on a variety of subjects and prepared for different age groups.

KEY SKILLS

(S&L) Respond and restructure

(R) Respond to factual and informative texts

(W) Write in non-literary ways

(W) Use presentational devices

(W) Understand the writing process

PROGRESSION

Look for individual student progression in:

• the ability to summarise or generalise about aspects of information writing

• an understanding of audience in the preparation of materials

• a concern for attractive and accurate presentation that communicates effectively.

USING THE UNIT

1 Read an information book

There is often a temptation to describe any non-literary text as non-fiction but this categorisation is not really helpful to students. The information books described in this unit are non-fiction books that present factual information. Look in any school bookshop or a well-equipped library to see what an important share of the book market this kind of writing now commands. In many ways, it is a new type of writing. It differs from an encyclopedia entry in possessing much more awareness of the audience and in assuming that the knowledge it communicates is not interesting for its own sake but must be made interesting to the reader.

The discussion of the pages, use of the Skills box and the student's work can take place in any order. Some pupils will need to be talked through the pages and to work specifically on them. Others will be keen to work outwards, testing the ideas contained in the Skills box against other texts.

Talking is an important element in this because it should give individuals the opportunity to show how far they understand the form of the writing. Talking about a book in this way can help more diffident speakers to express a point of view.

Able pupils should provide a more detailed commentary on their reading. Copymaster 20 supports this activity.

2 Write your own information booklet

The steps for success support this task in detail, and underline that the task is quite complex. The approach is likely to vary depending on whether the class has access to wordprocessing and DTP facilities. If these are not available, then the pages can be coloured to add a new dimension to the presentation.

If students are stuck for ideas, suggest that their booklet should be one of a series, 'How it's done…' or 'The easy way to…'.

This task can clearly be developed into an extended piece of work. If less time is available, the booklets can be produced as a pair, or small group, endeavour.

The Tips box emphasises that even with limited wordprocessing facilities, it is still possible to use text effects. You could also use aspects of the Getting into Print unit in *English Solutions* book 1 to support this activity.

3 Check the results

Evaluation is a key element in improving writing. If the child test is impractical, another way to do this is to ask the class to review each other's work. The *Times Educational Supplement* is a handy place to find short reviews of this kind of material as exemplars.

EXTENDING THE UNIT

1 Read around the subject

Look at four or five information books, studying *how* they communicate information to the reader. Then, decide with a partner on the ten most important things for writers of information books to think about as they write. Compare your list with those drawn up by other pairs.

2 Find the best information book

Pick the book that you think is best at providing information. Talk to the class about why it should win the class award for best information book. After everyone has done this, take a vote to find a winner.

3 Apply what you have found out

Use what you now know about information writing to produce a booklet based on your work in another school subject. Write it so that it can be used by you – or your friends – to revise what you have learned about a topic for an end-of-year test.

Factbooks
Writing a book review

Write a book review of the information book which you think is the best. Follow these steps for success:

1 Say what the book is called and who it is by. You can do this in a number of ways.

> Steam Power by Jessica Rood.
> Felixstowe Publications 1995.
> This book provides an excellent introduction to a fascinating subject.

> In Steam Power, by Jessica Rood, we find the history of steam explained with superb colour pictures and detailed explanations.

2 Write about the book's strongest features. This could be something to do with its content, layout or style.

> It is the mixture of diagrams and information that makes this book so informative. The book is very colourful and the writer clearly knows her subject. Miss Rood describes a complicated history in simple terms.

3 Then, either write about the content, layout and style in separate paragraphs or make a series of points about aspects of these. Bear in mind the interests and age of the readers as you write.

> The content of the book covers the development of steam engines from earliest times. However, there is a special emphasis on steam locomotives and the giant engines designed for the vast distances travelled in the United States and southern Africa.

> The language of the book is always kept as simple as possible even where complicated information is being given. Developments like the Caprotti valve gear, double chimneys and automatic firing are clearly explained and the diagrams and photographs are well-chosen and given plenty of space on the page.

4 Write a short conclusion summing up your views about the book and whether you would recommend it for a particular reader.

5 Redraft and produce a neat, accurate final version.

Rhyme and rhythm

AIMS

✔ This unit offers the chance to work with an anthology of materials in a number of ways.

✔ The poems are accessible and drawn from a range of cultures and times.

✔ Students are shown how to analyse rhyme schemes and rhythms in poetry.

ADDITIONAL RESOURCES

This unit will benefit from the collecting and reading of other rhyming poems. Audiotapes of poems are widely available and will also be useful.

KEY SKILLS

(S&L) Structure talk for an audience

(R) Read poetry

(R) Engage with content and language

(W) Write poetry

PROGRESSION

Look for individual student progression in:

• the ability to present an expressive reading of a chosen poem

• an understanding of why rhyme and rhythm are used by the poet and the effects he or she achieves

• confidence in brainstorming ideas

• the writing of poems where rhyme and rhythm are integral.

USING THE UNIT

1 Looking at poems

The poems in this unit will all benefit from a lively reading. Clearly, some of the poems are more accessible than others and the ability of the group will provide the best indicator of where to start.

Reading one or two poems and opening the discussion is probably the best way into the unit. Then, the students can read others in pairs or small groups, taking turns to read. Emphasise that these are poems to be read aloud with gusto!

How the writing and reading tasks that follow are used depends on the abilities of the class. Able students should be able to move directly into writing but others will need support or may be more confident in a group discussion.

Emphasise that the readings should make the poems come to life. Point out how a shared reading can bring different voices into a poem like *Father William*.

2 Present a song to the group

There is a shift in gear in the unit at this point. The Skills box presents some complex material and it may go into too much detail for some pupils. However, this kind of analysis is a useful technique for students.

The introduction of Shakespeare's songs is one way of introducing his work to all students. The Tips box supports the task. If the group is struggling with this, make it a class exercise. An audiotape recorder, a bell wrapped up in a fire blanket, ten pupils imitating the sea, two as seagulls and a couple of readers will produce an interesting result. Split larger classes into two and carry out the exercise twice to introduce a whiff of competition.

3 Write a rhyming poem

The Shakespeare theme continues here but as subject material for the students' own poems. The Tips box shows the group how to brainstorm: this is a handy skill in other situations and should provide plenty of material.

It is always satisfying to find an audience for work of this kind. One way is for the group to create its own anthology. Attractively presented, using DTP facilities and photocopied on coloured paper, an anthology of rhyming autumn poems for parents to see would send some positive messages home at the end of the autumn term.

EXTENDING THE UNIT

1 Collect more poems

Use poetry anthologies to find another example of a rhyming poem that you particularly like. If the poem is quite short, copy it out neatly. If longer, copy out some of the verses you particularly like. Now:

(a) Say what the poem is about and what you like about it.

(b) Copy out ten lines from the poem. Use what you have found out about poems to analyse the rhyme and rhythm in the poem.

(c) Imitate the rhyme and rhythm in a similar poem of your own – it does not have to be on the same subject.

2 Listen to music

Rhyme and rhythm are an essential part of songs and music. Find the words to a pop or rock music song where rhyme and rhythm are used for effect. Play the music to the class and describe how the music uses rhyme and rhythm.

3 Perform a poem

Take one of the poems from the unit and perform it with music, dance or sound effects. If you feel shy about this, make a tape of your poem where the reading is backed up with music and sounds.

4 Find the rhyme

Use Copymaster 21 to work out the rhymes in a poem by John Clare.

Rhyme and rhythm
Find the rhyme

Read this poem by John Clare. The final word in each line has been removed.
Using what you now know of rhyme and rhythm, decide which of the words in
the box should be used to complete each line. The word left over gives you
the title of the poem.

The snow has left the cottage …
The thatch moss grows in brighter …
And eaves in quick succession …
Where grinning icicles have …
Pit-patting with a pleasant …
In tubs set by the cottage …
While ducks with geese, with happy …
Plunge in the yard pond brimming …

The sun peeps through the …
Which children mark with laughing …
And in the wet street steal …
To tell each other spring is …
Then, as young hope the past …
In playing groups they often …
To build beside the sunny …
Their spring time huts of sticks and …

The barking dogs, by lane and …
Drive sheep afield from foddering …
And Echo, in her summer …
Briskly mocks the cheering …
The flocks, as from a prison …
Shake their wet fleeces in the …
While following fast, a misty …
Reeks from the moist grass as they …

again
been
brimming
broke
door
draw
drop
eye
February
green
ground
joys
mood
nigh
noise
o'er
recalls
run
smoke
sound
straw
sun
top
walls
window-pane
wood

Who's at home?

AIMS

- ✔ The unit explores the importance of succinct communication and layout in the writing of leaflets.
- ✔ It encourages the study of non-literary materials.
- ✔ It provides an opportunity to introduce other work based on aspects of crime prevention.

ADDITIONAL RESOURCES

Other leaflet materials will be helpful to show the possible range. Libraries, local pressure groups and the inside pages of newspapers and magazines are all sources for leaflet material.

KEY SKILLS

(S&L) Reach conclusions through discussion

(R) Respond to factual and informative texts

(W) Write in non-literary ways

(W) Use presentational devices

(W) Understand and use standard English

PROGRESSION

Look for individual student progression in:

- the ability to discuss the relationship between a message, style and layout
- presentational competence – perhaps using DTP facilities

USING THE UNIT

1 Look at an information sheet

Start this first task quickly. Allow students two or three minutes to study the material and then ask them to turn over the books and find out what has been absorbed. Ask more able students to list five clear recommendations.

The next tasks can operate as small group exercises where the requirement to reach a consensus on how to spend the money will focus the discussion.

2 Analyse an information sheet

This little information sheet has all the characteristics of a leaflet. With less able students this may be best undertaken as a class exercise. Otherwise small groups or pairs will be best. Introduce the topic and stress the need to be able to say something under each of the headings – words, illustrations and layout.

The commentary that follows should be a detailed piece of work. There are some complicated issues about audience and how to make people read things. The Skills box looks at the important and related issues of purpose and audience. Talk the group through this.

3 Design a leaflet

The final task is to design a shorter leaflet than the longer information sheet. Ask the group to think hard about the message. One way to do this is to write down what the leaflet has to say to people. This runs something like, 'Hello! Pick me Up! Notice Me! Read me quickly! Get my message! Read me more closely! Decide to do what I ask!'

Stress the importance of slogans, headings and text size in all of this. The unit asks for a colour leaflet – most are these days – but this could be sacrificed if DTP facilities are available. Also, black and white output from a printer can be very effectively coloured in and spaces left for illustrations. The Tips box stresses the messages about leaflets contained in this unit.

EXTENDING THE UNIT

1 Collect other leaflets

Find some other leaflets to compare. Look for leaflets:

- advertising shops and bargains that are included in local newspapers
- published by political parties at election time
- about local community issues
- produced by national campaign groups
- advertising local attractions
- advising people to be healthier.

Try to find one example of each. Then use what you know about leaflets to compare three of them, talking about purpose and audience and saying something about how they use words, layout and illustrations. Decide which leaflets are most effective and why.

2 Design another leaflet

Use what you now know to design and write one of the following leaflets:

- a leaflet advertising a charity fund-raising event at your school
- a leaflet arguing that a pedestrian crossing should be put on the busy road outside your school
- a leaflet to attract people to visit a local attraction in your area
- a leaflet warning people to leave their cars secure at all times.

3 Find out more about crime prevention

Invite your local community police officer into school to talk about local crime prevention schemes. Design and write a leaflet to help with this campaign.

The egg-man

AIMS

✔ This unit presents an extended extract from a short story and explores characterisation and viewpoint.

✔ There are opportunities for other kinds of work in analysing and extending the short story.

ADDITIONAL RESOURCES

Copies of the full story, from *Badger on the Barge* by Janni Howker, will be helpful. The Channel 4 television series for schools Middle English has also adapted this story for transmission in 1995 and 1996.

KEY SKILLS

(S&L) Contribute in discussion

(R) Read narrative

(W) Write narrative

PROGRESSION

Look for individual student progression in:

• the ability to empathise with the two girls in the story;

• an understanding of the egg-man's character on more than a superficial level;

• the ability to comment about character with confidence or to adopt an authoritative alternative viewpoint.

USING THE UNIT

1 The first meeting with the egg-man

There are various ways into a story like this. It is possible to preface the reading by talking about weird people with the class. Teenage students – preoccupied with their own emergent identities – are always very aware of odd characters and there will be plenty to talk about. However, such talk needs careful handling and local knowledge. Many teachers would prefer to let the reading speak for itself.

The discussion can be class-based, paired or in groups. It is a preliminary talk to reinforce the reading. The best written follow-up at this point would be to ask the class to make some notes on the characters of the egg-man, Bridget and Jane. Ask them, at the same time, to hazard a guess as to what might happen next.

2 Inside the egg-man's house

This extract and the next are dramatic scenes that will repay a teacher reading. The questions are set out as a reading comprehension but could be tackled through a discussion followed by a homework.

3 A conversation with the egg-man

Writing as another character is an important step on the way to the understanding that the attitudes of writers and their characters are different. The Tips box supports the activity. Talk about the need to sustain the changed viewpoint throughout the writing.

4 Write a character study

This task, with its steps for success, takes the student through an essential skill in literary study and it is well worth spending some time on this. The chart supplied should help but some students will need guidance as the redrafting takes place. A copy of the chart is supplied as Copymaster 22.

EXTENDING THE UNIT

1 Look more closely...

Working as a group, discuss your answers to these questions.

(a) Why are Bridget and Jane interested in the egg-man?

(b) What have you found out about Jane's family? Do you think that Bridget's background is the same?

(c) Has anyone in your group ever done anything similar? Why did he or she do it?

2 Role-play: daring a friend.

With a partner, improvise a situation where you dare a friend to do something that you know is wrong. Then, role-play a discussion between Bridget and Jane when they discuss whether to go back to the egg-man's house after their first visit.

3 Write a story

Either Start to write your own story about two schoolchildren who let their curiosity about an old person get the better of them.

Or Write about a time when you played tricks or spied on an old person.

4 Adapt the story for television

Read the description of the inside of the egg-man's house and then devise and draw the three-sided television sets you would need if you were to film this scene. Make them as detailed as you like. Add colour. As you work, think about the views that the camera might need to have.

5 Write a diary entry

Write Jane's diary entry when she looks back over the events of her half-term holiday.

The egg-man
Character study

As you find out information about the egg-man, make notes on this grid to help you complete your character study.

His face and head	His hands
His glasses and what he does with them	How he handles things
The way he speaks	How he keeps the house
How he walks	His way of life
The clothes he wears	How he reacts to the girls

A matter of taste

AIMS

✔ The unit introduces the study of advertising and explores some of the persuasive techniques used in the media.

✔ The focus on menus and food makes this a simple exercise that is accessible to all students.

✔ Features of persuasive language are introduced in an uncontroversial setting.

✔ There are opportunities to develop the unit into aspects of food technology.

ADDITIONAL RESOURCES

This unit can be linked to the unit called School Dinners in *English Solutions* book 1 to develop the theme of food. A collection of local menus will give the unit some local colour. Tapes of local radio advertising will support the main task. Audiotaping facilities are required for this.

KEY SKILLS

(S&L) Respond and restructure

(R) Engage with content and language

(R) Respond to factual and informative texts

(W) Write in non-literary ways

PROGRESSION

Look for individual student progression in:

• an understanding of persuasive effects and the idea of targeting a potential audience

• the ability to lead the group or to make constructive comment in the audiotaping exercise.

USING THE UNIT

1 Reading the menu

This is an ideal lesson for the last session of the morning! Local restaurants will normally be happy to give you their menus to support the exercise and to add local colour. This is useful to show how some restaurants make no effort to jazz up their offerings. It works best as a class exercise. Ask individuals to choose the most attractive options or to construct a three course dinner. Make it more complicated by inventing different audiences – an elderly vegetarian aunt, an American pen-pal, a foreign exchange student, a friend you want to impress and so on.

Talk the class through the Skills box on the language of persuasion before the discussion continues. The focus here should become more objective in approach. After a class follow-up session to share conclusions, a piece of written work commenting on the menus could be appropriate.

2 Write your own menus

This task blends creativity with an understanding of possible audience. The Tips box on selling points should help the planning of the menu. This will work well as an exercise for pairs of students, but larger groups are likely to get bogged down. Point out how a good menu offers choices that complement one another and also make clear that successful restaurants do not always have to be expensive or snobbish. Copymaster 23 supports this task for less able pupils.

3 Write a radio advertisement

The continuing success of independent local radio is likely to encourage the making of advertisements like these. Taping a series of advertisements will show the class how restrictive this medium is and how creative some of the current advertising is.

The Tips box offers some basic support for young producers. A dubbing facility (putting one sound on top of another) and an external microphone will greatly improve the quality of the finished product.

EXTENDING THE UNIT

1 Collect other menus

Find as many restaurant menus as you can – always ask politely. Compare the ways that each one tries to attract and encourage the potential purchaser.

2 Fast food

Plan a restaurant chain to compete with Macdonalds. Decide on your theme, plan your menus and finish off by designing the buildings, the colour scheme and the staff uniforms.

3 Selling points

The Tips box on page 81 lists some of the selling points that encourage people to choose restaurants. With a partner draw up what you think are the selling points that would encourage people to buy one of the following:

- a new car
- a holiday in the sun
- a portable stereo

Compare your decisions with those made by the rest of the class.

A matter of taste
Your own menu

Put the name of your restaurant at the top and then write your choices for each course in the spaces below:

Super Starters

_____

_____

_____

_____

Main Courses

_____

_____

_____

_____

_____

Lovely Sweets

_____

_____

_____

_____

Invent a language

AIMS

✔ The unit encourages students to reflect on the range and variety of language.

✔ It underlines the notion that all languages are rule-based systems.

✔ It is designed to be accessible to all students but to allow differentiation at all stages.

✔ It can be extended into more formal work on language structure and grammar.

✔ It can be used to link work in modern languages with English lessons.

ADDITIONAL RESOURCES

Examples of other languages will be useful, as will some basic phrasebooks or textbooks in other languages. Magazines and teenage fiction may provide examples of codes and versions of slang.

KEY SKILLS

(S&L) Contribute to discussion

(S&L) Understand the development of language

(R) Engage with content and language

(W) Write in non-literary ways

PROGRESSION

Look for individual student progression in:

• a willingness to talk about language in an objective way

• the understanding that language codes are systems based on rules

• an ability to invent and describe aspects of a language

USING THE UNIT

1 The rules of Arjy Parjy

The unit starts by looking at a well-known example of a private language, as described in Keith Waterhouse's book, *There is a Happy Land*. Working in pairs, many classes can go straight into this without any further introduction. Ask the pairs to show when they have finished by saying, 'We have finished our reading' in Arjy-Parjy.

The next task is more difficult but the Tips box should help the pairs to come up with three rules. They should be something like:

1. The phrase 'arj' is inserted once into some of the words in a sentence

2. The phrase is inserted only where a consonant is followed by a vowel sound

3. The phrase is not inserted into words of one or two letters

2 Languages of your own

Arjy Parjy is a genuine code used by children about which little seems to be known. In linguistic terms, its sing-song structure makes it close to a cant, like some of the modern sing-song dialects popular with black American rappers. Parjy is evidently a derivation of parler (to speak) and there was an 18th-century argot known as 'Parlyaree' associated with sailors, actors and the underworld. Perhaps, Arjy-Parjy was a child's attempt to reflect this private language.

There are other codes where syllables are inserted into words and many students will know of backslang or something similar. This unit does not try to separate out argots from private languages, codes or slang, although linguists might prefer to. The emphasis is that people who speak like this – for whatever reason – must be following some rules.

3 An invented language

Esperanto is, of course, a much more complicated language than this page might suggest. However, these particular aspects are simple and quite easily mastered. Able children will enjoy working out the translation individually while others will find it helpful to work in pairs or with some support. Point out to the group how the derivations in Esperanto from other languages help to make it easier to follow.

4 Invent your own language

This is quite a challenging exercise and can become very complicated. Stress that this is a language – like an argot – designed for a small community and a limited environment. Underline the need to keep the vocabulary school-based at the start. Also, point out that the language should be oral and that words with links to other languages studied,

slang or shared jokes and meanings will be much easier to remember. The Skills box provides some basic information on English parts of speech that may support some pupils. Talk the class through this before they begin to work on their languages in detail.

5 Write a language textbook

This exercise is for students who have become embroiled in the unit. Those who have developed a sophisticated slang and practised it will enjoy the task. An alternative would be to talk about how the group's modern language textbooks present the language, or languages, studied in school.

EXTENDING THE UNIT

1 Research other languages

Find out what you can about one of the following:

- cockney rhyming slang

- rap

Look in language encyclopedias and at record sleeves and inserts. Report back to the class.

2 Find out more about Esperanto

Look in your local library for an Esperanto textbook. Find out how the language came to be written and what some of the other rules are. Write up your findings as a short project or report back to the class.

3 Write a story

Write a short adventure story where two children escape from capture by using Arjy Parjy.

4 Write a playscript

Write a scene from a play where the characters all speak different slangs and codes. Make it a comedy.

Stranded

AIMS

✔ This unit gives an opportunity to study extended extracts from fiction including pre-twentieth century examples.

✔ A thematic grouping of the texts means that comparisons and contrasts can be made between the texts studied.

✔ The common theme can be extended to introduce the study of other texts.

ADDITIONAL RESOURCES

The complete text of *Treasure Island*, or film versions of *Swiss Family Robinson* and *Treasure Island* will be useful as will other related texts such as *Robinson Crusoe, The Tempest* and *Lord of the Flies* from which short extracts can be read.

KEY SKILLS

(S&L) Respond and restructure

(R) Read narrative

(W) Write narrative

(W) Understand and use standard English

PROGRESSION

Look for individual student progression in:

• an understanding of the extracts and subsequent discussion

• the ability to talk perceptively about what is read

• indications of control over, and the conscious structuring of, imaginative narrative.

USING THE UNIT

1 Look back on your reading

Most groups should come up with some stories. Apart from those listed, mention may be made of *The Island of Doctor Moreau* (Wells), *Sinbad the Sailor* (Arabian Nights), *Cyclops and Circe* (Greek mythology), *The Blue Lagoon* (film) and *Castaway* (film). Extend the discussion to the modern equivalent of the desert island – the lost spaceship or the unknown planet – and the numbers will increase. Make the point that it was quite possible to die on a desert island, or at least to land on an uninhabited one, until well into this century. Build up the notion of the desert island as the unknown, as nature – red in tooth and claw – and, of course, as the Garden of Eden.

2 Read the stories

Although they can be read in groups, 'The death of the donkey' and 'Jim's shore adventure' will often benefit from being read by the teacher. The first is a powerful description that paints a horrible scene. Ask the class what makes this so frightening. The answer lies in the sense that evil is lurking somewhere around the family, that the island is not entirely friendly and that the serpent is a threat to them all. It is also the snake in a metaphorical Eden and can be related to the alien in the eponymous film or to the dead airman in *Lord of the Flies*.

The second extract may need some context. The piratical plotters realise they have been discovered when they reach the island. On the pretence of visiting the island for other reasons, they set out to kill the crew members who oppose them. In this extract, Long John Silver, the pirates' leader, does his bit to help. The comparison of these first two extracts should draw out some similarities in the events and the setting.

'Crusoe's canoe' will also benefit from a teacher reading with some classes but the final extract, 'The boat', can be passed back to groups or pairs. This will give the class some sense of ownership over the unit and reinforce the discussion that follows. With some groups, this could be a written exercise.

Copymaster 24 provides comprehension questions on the extracts.

3 Tell a story through someone else's eyes

This task leads the extract into empathic accounts and the writing of imaginative narrative. Take the class through the writing process and the Tips box, underlining that a fully-finished piece of writing is required.

EXTENDING THE UNIT

1 Extend one of the stories

Write about another event through the eyes of either Fritz or Jim, where the sense of their horror and powerlessness comes through to the reader.

2 Read a novel

Find and read the opening chapters of *Swiss Family Robinson*, *Treasure Island* or *Robinson Crusoe*. Explain to the class how either the family, Jim, or Crusoe found themselves stranded.

3 Adapt an extract

Take one of the extracts in this unit and turn it into either a strip cartoon story or, if you are working as a group, a radio play.

Stranded
Questions on two of the extracts

Look closely at 'The death of the donkey' and then answer these questions:

1. How did the family know that the serpent was still in the area?

2. Why was the situation becoming 'critical'?

3. What do you think Falcon's Nest is? What clues tell you this?

4. How did the family's plan go wrong?

5. Why did Mr Robinson not try to save the donkey?

6. What impression do you get of the death of the donkey? What does it make you feel about the serpent?

7. Why, at the end of the extract, is the serpent 'powerless'?

8. Using a dictionary find the meanings of each of the words below. Choose another word or phrase that could replace it in the passage.

    Grotto (line 2)   fodder (line 26)   enveloped (line 70)
    nimbly (line 86)   stupor (line 135)

Look closely at 'Jim's shore adventure' and then answer these questions:

1. List five details that tell you that Jim is in a strange, and unknown, place?

2. What told Jim that he was not alone?

3. What does Silver mean when he says he thinks 'gold dust' of Tom? Do you believe him?

4. How does Tom argue that Silver should not take sides with the pirates?

5. Why does Jim call Tom, 'an honest hand'?

6. What does the fight at the end tell you about the character of Long John Silver?

7. Using a dictionary, find the meanings of each of the words below. Choose another word or phrase that could replace it in the passage.

    Undulating (line 8)   thicket (line 26)   anchorage (line 35)
    intruders (line 62)   simultaneous (line 100) destined (line 131)

Life in toyland

AIMS

✔ This unit encourages students to look back at the toys they owned in the past and at how toys are promoted in the present.

✔ It encourages them to appreciate how advertising may be aimed at various audiences.

✔ It can be extended into a discussion of gender stereotyping and the wider effects of advertising.

ADDITIONAL RESOURCES

Collections of toy advertisements will be useful. Mail-order catalogues and catalogues from companies like Argos and Toys'R'Us will provide examples of these, as will children's comics and magazines. Television is now a powerful advertising medium for toys, and video compilations of these will also make a contribution.

KEY SKILLS

(S&L) Reach conclusions through discussion

(R) Respond to factual and informative texts

(R) Engage with content and language

(W) Write in non-literary ways

PROGRESSION

Look for individual student progression in:

• the ability to see beneath the immediate surface of advertising materials

• competence in handling the discussions or in taking a subject forward

• the capacity to make objective remarks in a written analysis of an advertisement

USING THE UNIT

1 Look at toys – in the past and today

With some groups, this discussion may start as a whole class exercise. If so, end it by asking everyone to think hard about their favourite toy ever and then to be ready to describe it to the group. Alternatively, this can be a written home-work.

The quality of the discussion and reporting back of the answers about toys for boys and girls will lead to varied responses with different groups. More able students could write this exercise up into an extended piece of writing.

2 Advertising toys

As well as following up the previous section, the point of this task is to show that toy advertising is often not aimed at the consumer – the child – but at the purchaser – the parent or relative. Suggest that this should be a feature of the advertisements that the group design. Talk the group through the Tips box.

3 Analyse a toy advert

This task represents a jump to a more sophisticated level. The Tips box introduces advertising terms such as image, product and appeal. The meanings of these can be illustrated with other examples. For less able pupils, make this an oral exercise with lots of examples.

4 Thinking about wider issues

This is a chance to introduce a wider discussion of advertising with the group. The television advertising of children's toys is widely criticised for making children want what their parents cannot afford. Ask if there is really any difference between this kind of advertising and the rest.

EXTENDING THE UNIT

1 Collect some toy advertisements

As a group, make a collection of advertisements from comics and magazines. See if you can find other examples of toys where the advertising is aimed strongly at either boys or girls. Then, find examples of advertising aimed at parents and grandparents.

2 Watch some television

If possible, videotape and then make careful notes on three television advertisements for toys. Note down exactly what happens and the effect that the different parts of the commercial are meant to have on the viewer. Think about the *image* given of the toy, who the advert *appeals* to and what its *selling points* are.

3 Selling computer games

Write as much as you can about the way that computer games are advertised and promoted. Think about advertisements in magazines and on television and about television programmes that show them. What image of the games do they try to put across?

4 Catalogue sales

Find a catalogue with toy advertising in it. Go through it, noting down the toy that is advertised and, if a person is seen using the toy, describe him or her. At the end, compare the descriptions. Do your results suggest that advertisers are guilty of gender stereotyping?

Scary moments

AIMS

✔ The unit discusses the issue of violence in the media and its effect on young people.

✔ It explores how a text is read differently in novel or film versions and changed by adaptation.

✔ The unit is based around a well-known film, *Jurassic Park*, which is accessible to students at all levels.

✔ The unit could also be used to introduce a wider discussion of science fiction.

ADDITIONAL RESOURCES

The videotape version of *Jurassic Park* will make a major contribution to this unit. Copies of the book might also be made available.

KEY SKILLS

(S&L) Structure talk for an audience

(S&L) Respond and restructure

(R) Read narrative

(R) Engage with content and language

PROGRESSION

Look for individual student progression in:

• the ability to take the lead in discussion, inviting contributions and rephrasing what is said

• understanding that reading and film each involve a different sort of interaction with a text

• the ability to make a persuasive speech in a debate.

USING THE UNIT

1 Looking back at *Jurassic Park*

This film has been one of the greatest box office successes of all time. That in itself makes it worth studying. It is also interesting because it is based on an idea with its roots in science rather than dependent only on special effects. In fact, it is a good example of the SF genre. The book is less well-known but, if you have not come across it, you will see from the extracts that it is better written than you might expect! It was written some time before the film was made.

The unit starts with a chance to let off some steam about the subject. The group will be well aware of the current law on video rental which does not allow school students to hire a whole range of videotapes. Conversely, they will therefore be only too keen to discuss the ones they have seen! Draw the focus of the discussion back to what scared them as children and what sent them behind the sofa or kept them awake at night.

The reading of the extracts is probably best done by the teacher. Many students will recognise these scenes from the film – they are both highlighted there. The paired discussion that follows should lead to a reporting back session for the class.

2 Discuss screen violence

The focus of the unit shifts here to the presentation of ideas. The students need to recognise that merely describing their own reactions is not enough. With some groups this could be a full-scale debate but many students will prefer a chance to air their views in a more relaxed setting. Talk the group through the Tips box, illustrating the tips as you do so.

EXTENDING THE UNIT

1 Read *Jurassic Park*

Get hold of a copy of the novel *Jurassic Park*. Find out why Tim is waiting by the fence that rings the park and why the fence is no longer electrified.

2 Could it really happen?

The film was advertised as something that could really take place. Research the issue. Find out what you can about the scientific argument put forward in the film. Ask your science teacher to help you and use the library for further research.

3 Find out about science fiction

Jurassic Park is an example of science-fiction – a story which, if science progresses in certain ways, just could come true. See what you can find out about what happens in the following science-fiction films and stories:

The Time Machine

Total Recall

Back to the Future

War of the Worlds

Terminator

4 Write your own scene or story

Write your own opening chapter for *Jurassic Park 2*, the sequel, or describe how the film version will begin.

Listen up!

AIMS

✔ This unit focuses on listening abilities.

✔ It encourages self-evaluation by students.

✔ It fosters role play and interview skills.

✔ The unit can be extended by observing gender influences on talk.

ADDITIONAL RESOURCES

The unit requires audiotape to be used and will benefit from videotape facilities. Videotaped television discussion programmes or live interviews will allow the lessons of the unit to be exemplified.

KEY SKILLS

(S&L) Listen carefully and positively

(S&L) Reach conclusions through discussion

(S&L) Respond and restructure

(S&L) Structure talk for an audience

(W) Write in non-literary ways

PROGRESSION

Look for individual student progression in:

• a recognition that listening is interactive

• attempts to alter behaviour

• understanding how other people listen.

USING THE UNIT

1 Check how well you listen

This questionnaire is partly for fun but it has a serious purpose. It is best completed in pairs or in small groups. Remind the groups to score their responses on paper, not on the books! Afterwards, leave time for the groups to discuss their results and to consider whether the picture given of individuals matches their own, and their classmates', views.

2 How to improve your listening skills

Before starting this exercise talk the group through the Tips box, illustrating the points it makes. Then, the role play exercise needs about a lesson to complete. If it is feasible, stage an entertaining example with the help of a teaching colleague before the group starts work. As the group carries out the exercise, select a few examples to show the whole class. Ask the group to identify what is going wrong and what could be done better.

3 Interview a friend

This interview can be very informal but could also be used to provide videotape evidence for a department portfolio developed as part of your Key Stage 3 assessment process. Videotaped records of group work are largely inaccessible when standards are discussed, but these interviews could supply some useful indicators of success in prepared talk. If the records are to be used in this way, give the pairs more time to prepare for them, but do not necessarily encourage a full-scale rehearsal, as that will tend to make the responses artificial.

4 Find out if girls and boys talk differently

This discussion about talk is supported by the poem by Liz Lochhead, the inspectors' comments and the two Tips boxes. Again, it provides a chance to assess speaking and listening performances and to incorporate some assessment of the students' abilities in commenting on the language of the discussion. The latter is a difficult aspect of the national curriculum to exemplify.

Listen up!

Observing one another in the classroom is quite hard for students to do. If the level of concentration is unlikely to be achieved, ask the groups – after their discussion is finished – to evaluate what they think of one another as speakers and listeners.

5 Compare your findings

This is a chance for the group to review what has been learned by putting it into action. Suggest that the discussion takes place as a 'model' speaking and listening exercise. Draw the rules out of the discussion or set the writing of them as a homework to follow up the unit.

EXTENDING THE UNIT

1 Watch television

Watch the way that television interviewers work. If possible, videotape a few minutes of a live interview – not an edited one – to study. See how many of the listening skills that you have found out about are used by professional interviewers.

2 Interview someone else

The important thing about interviews is to understand that everyone has something interesting to say. It could be about their life history, their interests or their views. If possible, videotape or audiotape your interview. Afterwards, assess your own listening skills.

3 Devise a survey

Working as a group, devise a ten question survey that will show the readers of a teenage magazine whether or not they are good speakers. Do they think before opening their mouths? Do they change the way they speak according to their situation? Can they speak confidently in public? And so on.

Listen up!
Watching people talking

Observer sheet about (Name)

Discussing (Topic)

Observed by (Name)   **Date**

Observer's comments

Supportive listening

Eye contact	Body position	Expression	Encouraging words	Asking for explanation	Involving others	Rephrasing/ summarising

Competitive talking

Interrupting	Offering new opinions – and repeating them	Arguing/disagreeing	Ignoring other people's contributions

Observee's comments

CD covers

AIMS

✔ The unit focuses on the presentation of information on compact disc boxes.

✔ It encourages discussion of how packaging influences purchases.

✔ Designing a box cover helps develop presentational skills.

ADDITIONAL RESOURCES

Other CD boxes will be a valuable additional resource. Alternatively, the inside sleeves can be photocopied. Glossy music magazines carry colour advertisements that show recent CD covers.

KEY SKILLS

(S&L) Contribute in discussion

(R) Engage with content and language

(R) Respond to factual and informative texts

(W) Write in non-literary ways

(W) Use presentational devices

PROGRESSION

Look for individual student progression in:

• the ability to view the CD box as a media 'package' designed for a purpose

• the retrieval of subtle information from the CD cover

• an integrated approach to the design of a cover.

USING THE UNIT

1 What makes people choose CDs?

This unit is designed to develop critical and evaluative skills within an area of the media that is likely to be highly relevant to young people. However, the observational, retrieval and critical skills it fosters go beyond the area of music packaging.

This is a group exercise. Some pupils will be happy to tell you that they have never bought a CD or audiotape in their life if asked as individuals! However, the exercise should be followed up with some group discussion. If you feel happy about the security implications, make this into a music session where students can play tracks from their most recent purchases and say why they chose to buy them.

2 Look at CD covers

A sample CD will support this discussion and should provide a brief introduction before the students go on to look at the boxes illustrated. With some groups, this could be a written exercise.

3 Look at the information on a CD

This exercise is deliberately detailed. The box of a typical CD carries an enormous amount of information and the class will enjoy unpacking this. Challenge the group to decode all the information and to say why it is there, as well as what it is. The emphasis should be on careful observation and retrieval.

4 Design your own box cover

The amount of detail researched in the previous section of the unit should enable the group to see that this is more than an artistic exercise. There is a need to make the box cover present a message in a co-ordinated way and to target this message for a selected audience.

The artwork can be supported by collage or clippings from teenage and music magazines. There are obvious opportunities to use IT in the design, but, if resources are limited, use one computer and printer as a word generator for groups and then cut and paste the final versions by hand. Work to a larger scale than the final box and then use a photocopier to reduce the covers to a typical size. This will give the box a professional detailed look.

There are opportunities here to work with the art department. The national curriculum in art is positive about the need to have purpose and direction in art lessons and colleagues will find this exercise valuable.

5 Choose a class top ten

This is a chance to talk about personal taste and also to reinforce the design criteria that underpin the unit. Look at the top three in terms of their relationship to the target audience, their exploitation of the medium in terms of shape and content requirements as well as for their aesthetic value. This will make for a lively exchange of views.

EXTENDING THE UNIT

1 Compare CD covers

Pick two CD covers, one for a classical CD and one for a pop or rock recording. Describe and compare them. Think about:

- how they use illustrations
- the layout, lettering and titles
- who they are aimed at
- how successful you think they are.

2 Pick your favourite CD cover

Decide on your favourite CD cover. Talk to the group about what you like about it and say exactly why it appeals to you.

3 CD research

Find out, and explain to the class, how CDs record and play back sound. Try to find out something about their increasing use in computing as well as for music.

4 Target a cover

Design a new cover for the reissue of a CD you particularly like. Make your cover reflect the music and the appeal of the artist or artists you have chosen.

CD covers
Choosing CDs

Look at the information on a CD. Note down what you find there under the following headings:

Looking at the whole box

Title _____

Artist _____

Song titles _____

When was the CD made? _____

Who mixed the music? _____

Catalogue number _____

Publishers _____

Looking at the insert

Length of the CD _____

What is on the cover? _____

What is inside? _____

Are there any pictures? _____

Are there any logos? Draw them.

Make a list of the names in the acknowledgements _____
_____

Are the lyrics printed on the insert? _____

Who wrote the words? _____

Who wrote the music? _____

How long is each song? _____
_____
_____

Is there any other information on the insert? _____
_____

Looking at the disc

What colour is it? _____

Does it have any writing on it? _____

Is the information on the disc repeated in the packaging of the CD? _____

CD covers
Designing a CD

Use these outlines to draw your CD design.
Use a new sheet of paper if you wish to design a separate insert.

Front cover

Back cover
and spine

Animal characters

AIMS

✔ The unit compares the ways in which animals are represented in fiction.

✔ Pre-twentieth century texts are included.

✔ The unit encourages comparative study.

✔ It explores a range of writing types.

ADDITIONAL RESOURCES

The complete texts of the books studied in extract form will support the unit, as will talking books and videotapes.

KEY SKILLS

(S&L) Contribute in discussion

(R) Read narrative

(W) Write narrative

PROGRESSION

Look for individual student progression in:

• the ability to read more complex texts

• engagement with issues in the extracts that are not connected with the narrative

• the development of comparative skills

• an emerging critical approach.

USING THE UNIT

1 Making animals into people

Start the unit with a brief discussion of animals in stories. Disney's *The Lion King* might provide a recent example if the groups are struggling. Then, read the fables. The Chaucer extract will need a dramatic reading to bring out the subtlety of Coghill's re-telling. The exercise that follows begins with

discussion, but the second half of the task may be written and could make a useful homework task.

2 Write a fable of your own

The first exercise is difficult to do well but most students should be able to see how a retelling of the *Chanticleer* story in a much simplified form is quite possible – even if they struggle to write a convincing fable. Pick out and read examples that locate the animal well in the school or use some of the animal characteristics from the box on page 29 in the student's book.

3 Showing animals as animals

The remainder of this unit unravels the different purposes for using animals in stories. In general, there is an overall truth that stories about animals say something about people and the human condition, but the following sections demonstrate this. The Kipling extract from *The Jungle Book* needs a teacher reading and a chance to talk about the story before the writing starts. While the language is quite hard, most students will know the story and the characters.

The extract from *Black Beauty* will require less support. Once again, the questions can form the basis of a discussion or can be written. There would be an opportunity to read the class a section from *Animal Farm* at this point. More able students could discuss the different treatment of Black Beauty and Boxer.

4 Making animals real

The attempt to take the animal's point of view is, perhaps, another point on a spectrum rather than a change of direction. Jack London's writing is very powerful and students will enjoy emulating it. The discussion and 'interview' can be extended to include the writers of the other extracts.

5 Talking about animal stories

6 Writing an animal story

This exercise allows students to pick up ideas from all of the extracts they have read. Encourage the group to think hard about the animal and the audience in particular. Making the animal 'real' and targeting an audience are key routes to success in this exercise. Stress the need to draft at an early stage and to proof-read final versions. This story could be assessed as part of a department's Key Stage 3 teacher assessment.

EXTENDING THE UNIT

1 Read another story

Choose another story where animals are the main characters. Read it and report back to the class.

2 Compare the stories

The extracts you have read in this unit treat animals in different ways. Compare the different pictures they give of the animal world.

3 Animals on film

Think about the portrayal of animals on film and television. Using examples, say how animals are shown differently from the way they are portrayed in books. What is there about film and television that makes this happen?

4 The real lives of animals

Pick an animal portrayed in one of the extracts from the unit and find out about its real life and habitat. Write a short project to report this information. Then, try to identify where the writer of the story used realistic information and where he or she used imagination in describing an animal.

Design and presentation

AIMS

- ✔ The unit explores aspects of presentation through poetry.
- ✔ The anthology includes pre-twentieth century writers.
- ✔ It supports the writing of poems that make use of textual effects.
- ✔ It teaches the use of simile and metaphor.

ADDITIONAL RESOURCES

Collections of poems where text effects are used will be useful. Often these are found in books for primary schools. DTP facilities will enable the group to experiment further.

KEY SKILLS

- (S&L) Respond and restructure
- (R) Read poetry
- (W) Write poetry
- (W) Use presentational devices

PROGRESSION

Look for individual student progression in:

- the ability to discuss how the poems use effects
- a capacity to identify where the words and the layout are integrated
- the writing of poems where shape or text effects are used to achieve a purpose that is not merely decorative.

USING THE UNIT

1 Thinking about presentation

With the emphasis on presentation in the curriculum at Key Stage 3, it is important to consider the range of features available to students in all their work. This unit flags the importance of legible handwriting, page layout and design, through a selection of poetry where the layout complements the words. This makes an important initial point. Layout and presentation are text features that enhance the words and are not decoration.

The opening discussion should reveal that public writing, writing where legibility is paramount, and private writing all make distinct presentational demands and invite choices from writers. The Skills box takes the unit in the direction of poetry. It is probably best introduced by the teacher and discussed with the class.

2 Looking at the form of poetry

3 Using presentation in poetry

The poems in this small anthology show a number of approaches to shape and presentation. Point out to the group how line length and typographical effects are both used in the poetry. The chart (Copymaster 28) underlines this and asks the class to think not only about what is done, but also about the effect – intentional, of course – upon a reader.

The Skills box 'Aspects of presentation' gives some examples of textual effects and makes the point that they are achievable in handwriting as well as in print.

4 Presenting your own writing

Sylvia Mark's poem 'Windigo' is introduced to stress again that writing comes prior to presentation. It rehearses similes because the student's use of similes in the next exercise may inspire some ideas about presentation as a consequence.

If students are stuck for ideas where presentation could feature, suggest the idea of one-eyed Cyclops, or an alien in the shape of a coiled worm or a boa constrictor. Copymaster 29 supports this. Suggest that individuals think about tails and wings as shape poems, heavy animals for bold fonts and upper case lettering and so on.

Much can be achieved with DTP programs but also much of what is possible is complicated and demanding in terms of computer use. Decisions here about what can be attempted from the Tips box will depend upon the resources available.

5 Reviewing your results

This is a crucial stage. It can be tied in with the selection of work for a display. Underline for the class how presentation and communication are inextricably linked.

EXTENDING THE UNIT

1 Find other examples

As a homework, find two or three examples of writing where the presentation is part and parcel of the meaning. Other poems, children's books and advertising will be good places to start.

2 Write a poem to shape 1

Write one of the following poems:

- a poem in the shape of a star about space travel
- a poem in the shape of a mountain about mountaineering.

3 Write a poem to shape 2

Use the copymaster to write a poem in the shape of a circle about:

- the Earth and its environment
- a snake
- problems that keep coming back.

4 Pick a poem to present

Find a poem you like in an anthology and present it as well as you can using textual effects.

Design and presentation

How poems are presented

Title of poem	How is the poem presented?	Why has the writer done this? What effect is he or she seeking?

Design and presentation
Writing a circle poem

Use this shape and make your poem fit it as closely as possible.

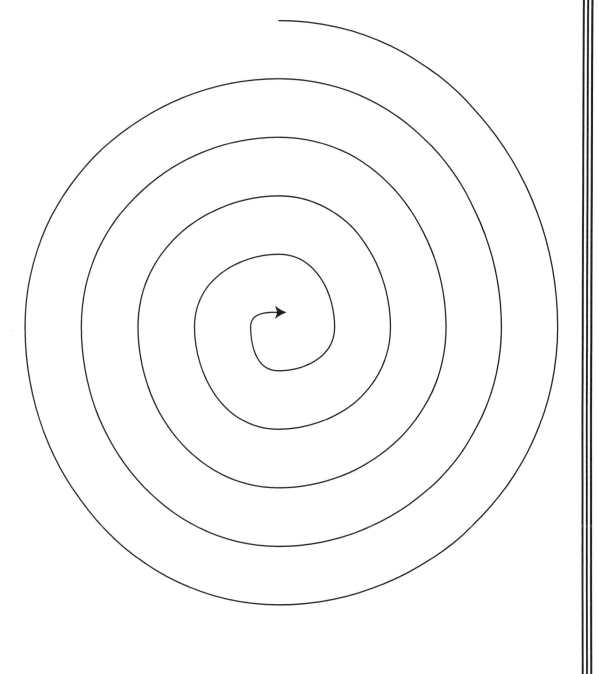

Shakespeare and his theatre

AIMS

✔ The unit allows the detailed study of extracts from three of Shakespeare's plays.

✔ It emphasises the importance of drama in performance.

✔ It introduces students to the Elizabethan theatre.

✔ The texts chosen are appropriate to national assessment at Key Stage 3.

ADDITIONAL RESOURCES

Full texts of the plays will be useful. Film versions can be used to show how directors approach the problems discussed in the unit. There are possibilities for model making and design that will require materials.

KEY SKILLS

(S&L) Reach conclusions through discussion

(R) Read plays

(W) Write in non-literary ways

(W) Write narrative

PROGRESSION

Look for individual student progression in:

• the reading and performance of the extracts

• the ability to comment about staging and positions

• the insight that movement is essential to the plot

• the recognition that a staged play has specific limitations.

USING THE UNIT

1 Inside Shakespeare's theatre

This unit is based on the idea that Shakespeare's plays were written to be performed in a simple theatre without curtains or scenery. It explores extracts from the recommended plays for Key Stage 3 assessment and provides an interesting way to investigate the dramatic qualities of the plays by looking at stage positions, spaces, entrances and extracts.

2 Look at *Julius Caesar* in performance

The key to this famous scene is: how can the conspirators be shown to be plotting against Caesar by the way they behave and move? It is important, of course, that anyone outside the circle of conspirators should not be able to hear them! The questions on the extract explore these issues. More able students will be able to write their answers, but with some groups a teacher-led discussion may be more appropriate.

3 Look at the setting for *A Midsummer Night's Dream*

The movement and placing of characters is central to this scene. It would be possible to identify a couple of key points to provide more focus for the task, although more able students should be capable of tracking all of the characters throughout the scene. Helena's lines, 'O, wilt thou darkling leave me? Do not so' and, 'Wherefore was I to this keen mockery born?' are good starting places for the exercise. Ask the group to decide who is on stage, and exactly where each of them is, at both these points.

4 Look at the duel scene in *Romeo and Juliet*

This is a more sophisticated exercise. The students are asked to map the scene and what happens. Models or plans will help to make this more effective. The extension task below suggests using mime. Another alternative is to act out the scene as if it is a modern day event, improvising language as necessary.

5 Perform an extract from a Shakespeare play

The main demand in this 'performance' is for action and movement. Talk to the group about the need to use these features to bring out the importance of the words and stress their importance in drama. Ask them to think about what they would see if they were an audience. This would be an ideal time of course to view one of the extracts on video or, better still, on stage.

6 Write as one of the audience at the Globe

This is a task that parallels the previous one putting the student in the audience. If a theatre visit is possible, a review of that event will be a useful comparison with this exercise.

EXTENDING THE UNIT

1 Putting *Julius Caesar* on television

In this extract from *Julius Caesar*, the conspirators are shown to be plotting against Caesar but the audience has to be able to hear what they say. How could you do this on television? Think about how television programmes and films show:

- that people are plotting a crime
- that they don't want to be overheard
- that they are anxious about plans that could put them in grave danger.

Present your ideas to the class.

2 Write about *A Midsummer Night's Dream*

At this point in the play, many of the relationships are in trouble! Write an agony column where Helena, Hermia, Lysander and Demetrius write in to air their problems. Give your Agony Aunt's replies.

3 Mime the duel scene for *Romeo and Juliet*

Having worked out the movements for this scene, mime what happens in slow motion. Don't speak but move around slowly to interpret the scene.

4 Research the time

Find out more about England in 1600 and the lives that people led. Write a brief project.

5 Shakespeare – the man

Find out what you can about William Shakespeare. Report back to the class.

Shakespeare and his theatre
The stage

Use this plan of the stage to map out the moves made by characters.

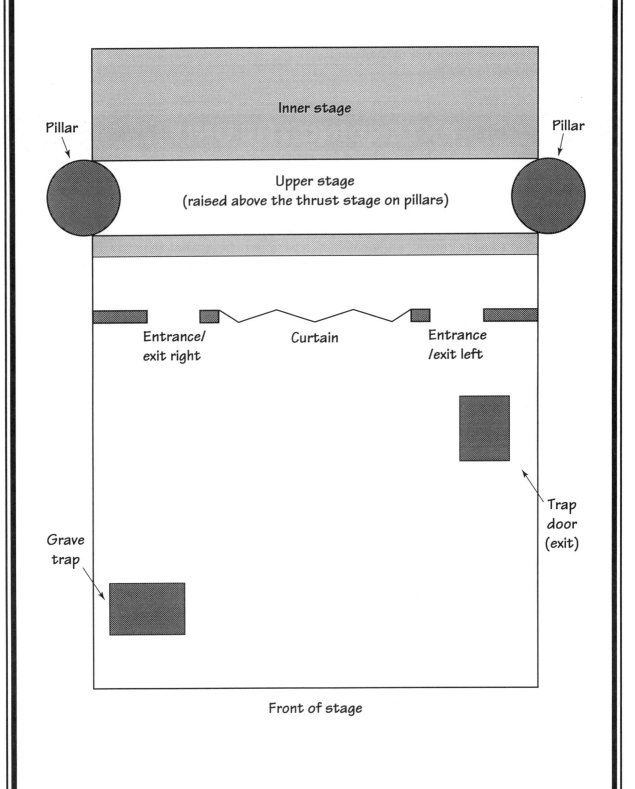

English Solutions   © Longman Group Limited 1995   **Book 3 unit 5**

The Harry Hastings method

AIMS

✔ This unit analyses the stylistic features of a short story.

✔ It studies the features of American English.

✔ It explores some of the issues involved in adaptations.

✔ The complete short story can be used in other ways.

ADDITIONAL RESOURCES

Other crime fiction collections, or examples of modern American magazine writing could be used to extend the unit.

KEY SKILLS

(S&L) Reach conclusions through discussion

(R) Understand the development of language

(R) Read narrative

(R) Engage with content and language

PROGRESSION

Look for individual student progression in:

● the ability to predict the ending of the story

● an awareness of the language used

● an understanding of the constraints that adaptation causes.

USING THE UNIT

1 Getting into the story

The reading of the story can be a class exercise that breaks down into groups of three for the subsequent discussion. The story is not demanding but it is quite long. Give the groups about ten minutes to think up alternative endings to the story. The questions on the story that end this section would make a useful homework task.

2 Looking at language and style

This task explores the minefield of language use, picking up on how this is an American text. Point out for the group how there are linguistic clues and informational clues and that these are separate.

3 Adapting the story

This exercise can be as complicated as required. View the letter as a starting point. Some groups, able pupils or those well-acquainted with media studies, may be able to offer a convincing full-scale treatment of the story. Storyboarding all or part of the story would also make an interesting task. Talk the group through the Tips box before the work starts.

The Harry Hastings method

EXTENDING THE UNIT

1 Harry Hastings

Using what you have found out from the story, write a short character study of Harry Hastings.

2 American English

Find another story by an American or other examples of American English. List the words that have a particular American meaning.

3 Watch television

Watch an episode from a television series you enjoy. Then, adapt the programme as a short story. As you work, ask yourself:

- what are you adding to the programme?
- what are the problems you face as you work?

Report back to the class.

4 Write a story

Write a story where a sequence of letters is a major feature of the plot.

American English

You could be quite surprised at the number of words that Americans use differently from us. Read the following passage and translate it into English!

I found the invitation to the party fixed to the bulletin board with a rusty thumb-tack. I checked the zip code and fetched some cookies and candy for the trip. My wife changed Elmore's diapers and found his pacifier. We grabbed a soda from the icebox, headed out of the apartment, into the elevator and then walked out onto the sidewalk.

I needed a flashlight to find the car in the darkness because the signs on the mall were turned off. I had to wrestle with the trunk as I put my bag in. The windshield was icy as it was only a week away from Thanksgiving and the Fall had come early.

I had picked up some gas and was just going down Main Street looking at the billboards and thinking about asking for a raise at work when this guy with a trailer swerved out of a side street and spun counterclockwise on the ice.

I braked hard and ran up against a streetlight and cracked the muffler. I hadn't even gotten to the freeway but at least I had his license plate.

_____

_____

_____

_____

_____

_____

_____

_____

_____

_____

_____

_____

_____

_____

It's the way that you say it

AIMS

✔ The unit explores contexts where standard English is appropriate.

✔ It presents a wide range of extracts for study.

✔ It focuses on the use of accent and dialect in prose and script.

✔ It shows how literary writing can often feature non-standard English.

ADDITIONAL RESOURCES

Videotapes of television programmes where dialect features will be useful. There are also several educational television broadcasts available that focus on aspects of accent and dialect.

KEY SKILLS

(S&L) Understand the development of language

(S&L) Listen carefully and positively

(S&L) Structure talk for an audience

(R) Read narrative

(R) Read plays

(W) Write script

PROGRESSION

Look for individual student progression in:

• the understanding that context influences talk

• an ability to distinguish between dialect and accent

• competence in reading aloud.

USING THE UNIT

1 Making judgements

This is best undertaken as a group activity. One way is to ask each person in a group of four to answer a question in turn before a more general discussion begins. Make time for a lengthy reporting back session and encourage the group to offer anecdotes about real situations.

2 How do you speak?

Writing a language history is an excellent classroom activity but it must be sensitively handled. A quiet word with the form tutor beforehand will ensure that pupils are not embarrassed. At the same time, it is important to stress that a varied language background is an asset in the modern world. The Skills box defines accent and dialect. Comment on this should be an important feature of the writing.

3 Other ways of talking

This should be an entertaining lesson. Pupils will realise quickly how many comics and how much television comedy plays with language out of context in these ways. Take the chance to discuss role play and how it relates to other drama.

4 Dialect in stories

The extract that starts this section is typical of a fiction genre that schools have to be aware of. Regional/historical/family sagas form an increasingly popular genre and many of the books feature dialect and accent in writing. This is an interesting piece for groups or pairs to read aloud, sharing the reading after a little preparation time. The discussion will reveal just how difficult it is to show an accent in writing.

5 Dialect in script

In some ways, dialect in script is easier to handle because the spoken words are clearly separated. This script is written in Jamaican Creole – the discussion of how a pidgin becomes a Creole is an interesting sideline.

6 Using dialect in your own writing

The writing of the script has to be a disciplined process and the Tips boxes should help with this. Go through them with the group before the writing begins. In an area where the local dialect is strong, this aspect could be expanded beforehand to look at that dialect in comparison to standard English. Encourage the group to use dialect and accent in different ways for different characters.

EXTENDING THE UNIT

1 Read a saga

Find a novel where accent and dialect are important features. Read it and retell the story to the class.

2 Write your own story

Write a continuation of Clem's story, where he goes back to the inn to find out more about the stranger. Use accent and dialect in the conversation.

3 Write about accent and dialect

How does the language of your area differ from standard English? Which words are pronounced differently? Are verbs changed? Are words put in the same order?

4 Play around with accent and dialect

Working as a group, practise reading the passage below (taken from a job interview) in a range of accents. Try the accents associated with public schools, BBC news-readers, Liverpool, Yorkshire, London, the West Midlands and the West Country. Discuss as a group how the meaning changes with the accent used.

> 'I'm afraid I didn't do well at school. In fact, it didn't agree with me at all. I left as soon as I could and decided to make my own way in the world. That's why I'm here looking for a job today. I have lots of work experience. I've been a waiter and worked as a farm-hand. Then there was the time I spent at Parkhurst Prison where I ran the Library. My uncle got me that job because he's been there for fifteen years. He's the governor and everyone respects him.
>
> I've travelled as well. I've been to Greece and Spain and have just come back from Monaco where I saw the Grand Prix.'

It's the way that you say it
Ways of speaking

Look at the different situations below and for each one tick the box that best describes how you would talk.

A   I would speak as I normally do
B   I would make changes to my dialect
C   I would make changes to my accent

		A	B	C
1	You are asked to show an important visitor round your school	☐	☐	☐
2	You need to return an almost new faulty personal stereo to a shop and ask for it to be replaced under the guarantee	☐	☐	☐
3	You are asked to read the news on national radio	☐	☐	☐
4	You are entertaining your friends with an account of a party you went to at the weekend	☐	☐	☐
5	You decide to put down someone who has been teasing you about your accent	☐	☐	☐
6	You are reading the weather forecast on breakfast television	☐	☐	☐
7	You have moved house to another part of the country, about two hundred miles away. In your class at your new school you are trying to get to know someone who seems to be very popular with the others	☐	☐	☐
8	A member of the Royal Family starts a conversation with you during a walkabout	☐	☐	☐
9	You are appearing on 'Blind Date' and you want to be the one who gets chosen	☐	☐	☐
10	You are invited to be guest DJ on your favourite radio music station	☐	☐	☐

English Solutions   © Longman Group Limited 1995   **Book 3 unit 7**

Good friends

AIMS

- ✔ This unit offers a range of extracts connected with the same theme.
- ✔ It engages with pre-twentieth century writing.
- ✔ It supports descriptive writing about characters.

ADDITIONAL RESOURCES

Videotape or film versions of *Tom Sawyer* and *Jane Eyre* will help to develop the unit and support its most challenging aspects.

KEY SKILLS

(S&L) Listen carefully and positively

(S&L) Restructure and respond

(R) Read narrative

(W) Write narrative

PROGRESSION

Look for individual student progression in:

- the ability to handle demanding reading material
- the capacity to deduce character from text
- the noting of language features.

USING THE UNIT

1 What is friendship?

This is a discussion to open up the issue of friendship and addresses the differences between friends of the same sex. There are possibilities here for some links with PSE and sex education.

2 Looking at friendships in literature

Mark Twain's stories are recommended reading for Key Stage 3 but can be quite demanding as pieces of reading. With some groups, a teacher reading will be helpful. The exercise that follows can be made more formal with some groups, or teacher-led where the passage has proved particularly challenging.

The extract from *Jane Eyre*, another recommended text, is possibly more difficult. Jane has been accused of telling lies by Mr Brocklehurst and the idea of standing by your friend is one that could be teased out of the reading.

The *Red Ball* extract is very different and raises the question of whether boys form different types of friendships to those formed by girls. It suggests that boys form larger, looser groups to which newcomers have to gain admittance, whereas Jane and Helen have a much more personal meeting arising, one might argue, from their common experience of cruel treatment by adults in the school. There is plenty to discuss here with able students.

3 Choose a fictional friend

The letter asked for here is a starting point for some – potentially – very sophisticated writing about character and attitudes. At the same time, it should allow less able students to express their opinions in a positive way.

Good friends

 EXTENDING THE UNIT

1 Read another book

Find and read another book or story where friendship is an important element. Tell the class about the friendship it describes.

2 Write a story

Write a story in three parts about how two people first become friends, have an adventure and then – later – stay friends or grow apart. Use the story to express your own view of friendship.

3 Look back ...

Write about a friend you remember from primary school but you no longer go around with. Describe him or her in detail and say how your friendship developed.

4 Soap friendships

Friendship is a major feature in television soap operas for young people. Using plenty of examples, write about how friends are portrayed in the programmes you watch regularly. Use the checklist at the start of the unit to help you.

Good friends
What is friendship?

A *good friend is* ...	1	2	3	4	5
1 Someone who likes the things that you do.	☐	☐	☐	☐	☐
2 Someone you admire.	☐	☐	☐	☐	☐
3 Someone who makes you laugh.	☐	☐	☐	☐	☐
4 Someone you can trust with secrets.	☐	☐	☐	☐	☐
5 Someone who is easy to talk to.	☐	☐	☐	☐	☐
6 Someone good looking.	☐	☐	☐	☐	☐
7 Someone who is generous.	☐	☐	☐	☐	☐
8 Someone who is sympathetic when you feel miserable.	☐	☐	☐	☐	☐
9 Someone who is popular with others.	☐	☐	☐	☐	☐
10 Someone who admires you.	☐	☐	☐	☐	☐

What other qualities might a good friend have?

_____

_____

Good friends
Looking at the language

What Tom admires about Huck

_____

The evidence from the passage

_____

_____

What Huck admires about Tom

_____

The evidence from the passage

_____

_____

Use this table to explore the language in **Tom Sawyer** and **Jane Eyre**.

The phrase from the story	Why you think this phrase shows the book was written long ago

Driven to the limits

AIMS

✔ The unit engages with an important social issue through imaginative writing.

✔ It develops notions of characterisation, plot and viewpoint.

✔ Drafting, redrafting and proofreading are emphasised.

ADDITIONAL RESOURCES

Other materials on so-called 'joyriders' may be useful. The local community police officer may also be willing to talk to the group about some of the consequences.

KEY SKILLS

(S&L) Reach conclusions through discussion

(R) Respond to factual and informative texts

(W) Write narrative

(W) Understand the writing process

PROGRESSION

Look for individual student progression in:

- the ability to see the opportunities in plot development
- competency in writing structured narrative
- an understanding of how viewpoint influences narrative.

USING THE UNIT

1 Starting your story

2 Create a character

This story writing unit presents an opportunity to discuss a serious social problem through work in English. However, its main focus is on the development of narrative skills. The opening discussion can take place with the whole class but it is recommended that it should start in groups.

If there is any tendency to trivialise the issue, it might be sensible to introduce the 'afterword' at some point in the discussion. The development of character is meant to be informed without creating a pathological picture of the car thief and this is an interesting balance to explore with the class. Current soap opera villains should provide models for discussion.

3 Develop the plot

This is a key part of the unit, offering storyline options to the group. This conscious process of plot development is often overlooked in schools, but it is an essential step in understanding that the plots of the novels studied in Years 10 and 11 are intentional. There would be an opportunity here to look at how to make notes about a plot – using a tree diagram or linked circles, for example.

Keep the writing collaborative at this stage so that ideas are shared, borrowed and adapted. Talk the group through the plot and sub-plot Tips box. Sub-plots are another underused feature of narratives written at this stage yet they are increasingly common in television drama.

4 Start to tell your story

5 End your story

Narrative viewpoint is something that often crops up in GCSE courses where novels are studied but it is rare for students to have a chance to practise using different viewpoints at an earlier stage. It is well worth doing because books and television take increasing liberties with viewpoint. Talk

Driven to the limits

the group through the Skills box, pointing out how the language (person, vocabulary, sentence length and register) reflects the chosen viewpoint.

All this should add up to a powerful stimulus. Give plenty of time for the writing to emerge because some of these stories may be quite lengthy. Stress that this should be a draft at this stage. Discuss endings at some point and stress the need for a good story to hold on to reality. The Tips box should also allow a discussion of alternative endings such as climax, anticlimax, build up and sudden endings.

6 Redrafting and proof-reading the final version

7 Afterword

Redrafting and proof-reading are skills that the curriculum emphasises. There is a tripartite approach to proof-reading used here that is worth fostering with students. It starts with 'global' modifications where the whole text is considered. Then, 'local' changes are made to add description, colour and variety before a final 'accuracy' check. Students often imagine that drafting is one of these and ignore the others!

Introduce and read the afterword here if that has not been done previously. Explore any links with PSE or opportunities to introduce an outside speaker as well.

EXTENDING THE UNIT

1 Car theft

Find out as much as you can about the increasing problems of car theft. Newspapers on CD-ROM will provide a useful source as will magazines. Interview your local community police officer and visit a local car dealer to see what car manufacturers are doing. Report back to the class.

2 Bad language

Joyriding is an odd expression for an activity that kills and maims so many people. Can you think of other words that sound nice but mean something worse? Begin by thinking about animals. Think about what the following mean:

culling	putting to sleep	snaring
neutering	baiting	hunting

3 Adaptation

Look at how your story might be adapted as a film for television by doing the following:

- describe how it would start and finish and how the most important scenes would be filmed
- write a short section of the script giving clear instructions about what the camera should see
- story-board the opening sequence.

4 Dramatise

With a group, create a short play about a family where one of the children steals cars.

5 Gender issues

Most cars are stolen by men. Discuss this fact as a group. You need to think about:

- why men do it
- whether women have a part to play
- what women really think about it
- what men think women think about it
- what are the solutions?

Driven to the limits
Design a poster

Use this outline to help you design a poster to be put up in every secondary school. It is intended to make teenagers aware of the dangers of driving in stolen cars. Think carefully about your slogan, what to put in the two written sections of the poster and what to have as your illustration. Make the final poster A3 size (twice as large as this sheet of paper).

PUT YOUR MAIN SLOGAN HERE

**Joyriding
– the facts**

*YOUR WRITING
GOES HERE*

ILLUSTRATION

What you can do to stop it

YOUR WRITING GOES HERE

YOUR SLOGAN CONTINUED OR ANOTHER MESSAGE

English Solutions © Longman Group Limited 1995 **Book 3 unit 9**

Animal crackers

AIMS

✔ This unit encourages students to collect together information about a subject.

✔ Students are helped to write letters to find out information.

✔ The unit supports the study and writing of persuasive magazine articles.

ADDITIONAL RESOURCES

Other magazine articles and examples of persuasive writing will be helpful. Some of the leaflet and material from campaign groups could be collected in advance. Classroom speakers from animal rights pressure groups will bring the unit to life.

KEY SKILLS

S&L Contribute in discussion

R Engage with content and language

W Write in non-literary ways

W Understand and use standard English

PROGRESSION

Look for individual student progression in:

• the ability to undertake independent research

• engagement with the issues at more than one level

• some understanding that persuasion is a type of writing with its own protocols

• the ability to construct a persuasive piece of writing.

USING THE UNIT

1 Look at what happens to animals

This introductory discussion provides a focus for the work that follows. The subject of animal use or abuse is a vast one and it is important that students take an overview. It is worth making the point that different nations take very different attitudes towards animals and that religious attitudes can play a part. The Japanese eat dolphins, dog is a delicacy in parts of Asia and the Norwegians kill whales. Cows are important to Hindus and pigs are disliked by Muslims and Jews. The Spanish like bullfights. Of course, we think we are more civilised, but English people kill wild animals in ways that would be highly offensive to people in Africa or India who have great respect for the animal world. There should be plenty to argue and disagree about and facts should not be in short supply.

2 Find out more about an issue

This part of the unit builds on the previous discussion. The students should now have points to make and be keen to find supporting information that will back them up. The Tips boxes and the Skills box go into the process of finding out in some detail. In an information laden world, students need more guidance on pathways to explore and more advice on being able to keep records and retrace their steps where necessary.

3 Looking at persuasive writing

Much of the writing that students will encounter in their research is persuasive as well as informative. These two articles provide a way of looking at how similar facts can be used to argue in two directions. The questions that follow the chart compare them in quite sophisticated ways. This could be a written task with more able students and is similar to the kind of task set in the extension paper for Key Stage 3 assessment in English.

4 Your turn to persuade

The unit closes with the chance to write an article on one of the subjects discussed. The advice parallels the advice on narrative writing in the previous unit but puts it in a non-narrative context. DTP facilities will be helpful in producing a neat final version.

EXTENDING THE UNIT

1 Find out more

Pick any one of the topics you have discussed in this unit. Write a short project about what happens where and give your views.

2 Look at both sides of an issue

Pick an issue and find material that supports both sides of an argument. Compare the case – for and against – and give your conclusion.

3 Write a letter

Write a letter to a national newspaper about one of the issues, setting out your views clearly and asking people to support you.

4 Monitor the papers

Spend a week reading the newspapers each day for 'animal' stories. At the end of the week review your evidence. Decide what sort of picture the newspapers give of our attitude to animals and report back to the class.

Animal crackers
Writing your letter

Use this page to help you write a letter. Fill in the spaces and then write a neat version to send.

Today's date

_____

Your name and address

_____

_____

_____

_____

The name and address of the people you are writing to

_____

_____

_____

_____

Dear Sir or Madam

I am interested in finding out some information about

_____

_____

_____

_____

_____

I hope that you can help me and send me any relevant leaflets. I enclose a stamped addressed envelope. If there is a charge for materials, then please send me a list of what is available.

Thank you for your help.

Yours faithfully,

_____